Bee Nilson was born in New Zealand and received her professional training there, graduating as Bachelor of Home Science from Otago University. After three years working in New Zealand she came to England and for more than thirty years has combined a full-time job with running her own home and writing books on cookery and dietetics. The development of her cooking has been influenced by her husband, who is an experienced traveller in Europe.

She has published many books on cookery, ranging from the classic *Penguin Cookery Book* to *Deep Freeze Cooking* and *Bee's Blender Book*, in which she delves into the more specialist use of modern kitchen tools, and *Bee Nilson's Slimming Cookbook*, in which her dietetic knowledge comes to the fore.

D1494448

Bee Nilson
B.H.Sc., S.R.D., Dip. Ed.

Bee's Blender Book

MAYFLOWER
GRANADA PUBLISHING
London Toronto Sydney New York

Published by Granada Publishing Limited in 1972
Reprinted 1973, 1976, 1977, 1980

ISBN 0 583 19739 6

First published by Pelham Books Ltd 1971
Copyright © Bee Nilson 1971

Granada Publishing Limited
Frogmore, St Albans Herts, AL2 2NF
and
3 Upper James Street, London W1R 4BP
866 United Nations Plaza, New York, NY 10017 USA
117 York Street, Sydney, NSW 2000 Australia
100 Skyway Avenue, Rexdale, Ontario, M9W 3A6, Canada
PO Box 84165, Greenside, 2034 Johannesburg, South Africa
61 Beach Road, Auckland, New Zealand

Made and printed in Great Britain by
C. Nicholls & Company Ltd
The Philips Park Press, Manchester
Set in Intertype Times

Contents

Introduction

IF one is lucky enough to have a blender or liquidiser it is a pity not to make full use of it. I consider the blender to be one of the best kitchen aids of our time.

While it is true that no special recipes and techniques are needed for blending simple things like drinks, for getting lumps out of sauces, or making purées, in order to use a blender to the full, some adaptations of methods and proportions of ingredients are needed.

At first I used mine as a tool for making quick and economical breakfast juices, for soups, and for anything requiring a purée, in short, as a labour-saver in conventional cooking. Gradually I began to adapt methods and amend recipes to make a fuller use of the machine. I hope some of these, and other of my recipes, will be new to you and will give you fresh ideas for using your blender, not only to cut down on preparation time, but to produce new types of food.

In selecting the recipes I have tried to confine my choice to those where the use of a blender either makes preparation quicker, really saves labour, or produces better results than are obtained by older methods. The recipes include some which are suitable for everyday catering and others for special occasions.

I would like to acknowledge the assistance I have had from manufacturers of blenders and liquidisers. Their helpful literature started me on my experimenting and provided many ideas for this book.

BEE NILSON

Chapter One

WEIGHTS AND MEASURES

ALL MEASURES USED IN THIS BOOK ARE LEVEL MEASURES

Quantities in the recipes are given in ounces, pounds, and pints followed by the equivalent amounts in grams, kilograms, litres or millilitres shown in brackets. These metric equivalents are only approximations and not exact conversions but they are sufficiently accurate to give good results, while at the same time being practical weights and measures suitable for using with metric kitchen scales and measures.

The tablespoon used in the recipes is a 15 millilitre spoon and the teaspoon is 5 millilitres, both being the same size as medicinal tablespoons and teaspoons.

British Weights and Measures

1 pound (lb.)	= 16 ounces (oz.)
1 pint (pt)	= 20 fluid ounces (fl. oz.)
¼ pint	= 10 tablespoons (Tbs)
⅛ pint	= 5 tablespoons

Metric Weights and Measures

1 kilogram (kg)	= 1,000 grams (g)
1 litre (l)	= 1,000 millilitres (ml) *or*
	10 decilitres (dl)

Conversion Table

1 ounce	= 28·35 grams
1 pound	= 453·6 grams (approx. ½ kg)
1 fluid ounce	= 28·41 millilitres
1 pint	= 568·2 millilitres (approx. ½ l)
1 inch	= 2·54 centimetres (cm) or 25·4 millimetres (mm)

Chapter Two

HINTS FOR NEW BLENDER USERS

Whether yours is called a blender or a liquidiser is immaterial; they all work the same way.

The blender consists of a goblet which is usually a little wider at the top than at the base, though one model on the market has a very wide base and narrow top.

The chopping, grinding, pulping, liquidising and blending is performed by stainless steel cutting blades attached to the base of the goblet which in turn slots into a base containing an electric motor. This is controlled by a switch, or in some cases by a push button. The motor base may be just for the blender or it may be one designed to power a mixer and attachments. As the blades in the base of the goblet revolve the mixture rises up the sides of the goblet and falls down the centre on to the blades which revolve at a very high speed and will chop, blend or liquidise depending on the length of time the motor runs and on whether or not liquid is added.

When the blender is first switched on, particularly if it contains something like hot soup, the initial swish of liquid against the lid can make it fly off and the contents splash out. It is a wise precaution to get into the habit of putting your hand on the lid when switching the motor on. After that it can be left, but most operations are completed in half a minute or less.

DIFFERENT KINDS OF BLENDERS

There are two main types available, one being an optional attachment for a food mixer, the other a free-standing blender with its own separate motor. A third variation consists of a combination of a small blender and beater.

The most expensive to buy is a large free-standing blender. If you already have a mixer it is cheaper to buy the blender attachment than a separate blender. On the other hand, it costs less to buy a free-standing blender then it does to buy a mixer plus blender attachment, and this has the advantage of being easier to store and can be left assembled for immediate use.

Goblet capacities vary from as little as $\frac{1}{2}$ pint for a small inexpensive one, to 2 pints or slightly larger. Naturally it takes longer to blend a fair-sized mixture in the small ones; you have to do it in several lots, but even this is so quick that it saves time when compared with other methods of mixing.

Blenders vary, too, in their performance. Most of them are good at making breadcrumbs, chopping nuts, pulping raw liver and cooked or raw vegetables and fruit, mixing drinks, and making mayonnaise. They vary in their ability to do other jobs.

The goblet is sometimes made of heat-resistant plastic, others are of heat-resistant glass. The glass ones are heavy and steadier to use but, unless you have strong hands and wrists, you will find those without a handle are difficult to hold for scraping out food, a necessary operation with thick mixtures.

The larger blenders have two or more speeds for doing different jobs, while the smaller ones usually only have one speed. It is an advantage, though not essential, to have a slow speed for chopping foods, as with fast blending it is easy to go too far and produce a pulp or grind instead of chopping.

If you are setting out to buy a blender or mixer it is advisable to study the latest reports published in "Which", the monthly magazine of the Consumers' Association, 14 Buckingham Street, London, W.C.2. From time to time they test and report on appliances of this kind.

HOW TO USE THE BLENDER

When buying a blender make sure you get an instruction book with it, because each model varies in some detail and it is important to follow the makers' instructions, at least until you are familiar with using the machine. The chief points to note are the recommended method of assembling and switching on, the way to fasten the lid securely, the quantities of food you can process at a time, and the best speed to use for different jobs. Some models have recommended speeds printed on the blender stand. Note, too, any special instructions for cleaning and care.

The amount of food you can process at a time will vary not only with your particular model, but also with the nature of the food. You will get to know the sound it makes and be able to judge when you have overloaded it. This either leads to a slowing down or stalling of the motor (to be avoided if possible); or the mixture won't circulate properly so that the bottom layer blends but the top remains untouched. The remedy is to tip out half and blend it later, possibly adding more liquid too. If you put in too small an amount it will be flung against the sides of the goblet and leave the motor racing (also to be avoided). For most foods there needs to be enough to cover the blades before you switch on, although when chopping dry goods like nuts less can be used. Never fill a goblet more than two thirds full of liquid, or more than half full with a thick mixture.

With small models it is usually inadvisable to run the motor continuously for more than one minute; two minutes with larger models.

Some manufacturers provide a plastic spatula for scraping out thick mixtures and dislodging foods stuck under the blades, but any long-handled plastic or wooden spoon with a small bowl is suitable. When blending a stiff mixture it is a good idea to retain a tablespoon or so of the liquid in the recipe and use this for swilling out the goblet to release food stuck on the bottom.

In general, the drier and thicker the mixture, the less can be processed at a time. For very thick foods it is better to use the on/off technique, repeating this until the food is mixed as required. This action helps to draw the food down on to the blades. With most foods, unless you are chopping dry ones, it is more satisfactory to put some liquid in the goblet first and with most it helps to cut the solid food in $\frac{1}{4} - \frac{1}{2}$ inch cubes ($\frac{1}{2} - 1$ cm). If ice is used it is usually better to crush it first although large blenders can deal with whole cubes of ice, and whole fruit and vegetables.

Be very careful not to allow any hard things like fruit stones or bones to get in by mistake as these are liable to stall the motor and damage the blades. If this does happen you will hear something is wrong as soon as you switch on, so switch off immediately and tip out the contents.

Sometimes better results are obtained when the motor is switched on before food is added, in this case through the top. Large models often have a small centre cap which lifts out to allow food to be dropped through the hole. With other models the whole lid must be removed and, if the food is dry and likely to fly about, you must keep one hand over the top while you feed in the food through a small gap. Sometimes part of a mixture is blended, then more ingredients are added with the motor running. In this case be very careful to switch off BEFORE removing the top or the contents will fly out and make a mess.

CLEANING

This is very simple and one of the things I specially like about using a blender is that the amount of washing up is reduced, when compared with making the same recipe the old way.

Simply half or two thirds fill the goblet with warm water, add a pinch of detergent powder or a few drops of liquid detergent if the contents have been greasy, sticky, or strong smelling. Put on the lid, switch on and run for 30 seconds. Tip out and rinse. Leave to drain upside down.

Some makes come apart for washing the blades separately from the goblet. This has the advantage that when solid foods have been blended you can inspect to be absolutely sure there are no particles remaining under the blades. This is particularly useful if you tend to leave the goblet standing after use and before cleaning. Be sure the parts are quite dry before you assemble for storage. Do not leave any make of blender with the lid tightly in place. Tilt the lid to allow air to circulate and moisture to evaporate. If you are not careful about this the goblet can develop a musty smell, especially if it is not in use every day.

Chapter Three

BASIC BLENDER METHODS

TO MAKE PURÉES

FRUIT

To purée firm fruit like unripe gooseberries, fresh apricots, firm bananas, apples or pears, add either water, fruit juice, evaporated milk or other liquid in the proportion of $\frac{1}{4}$ pt. liquid (150 ml) to 1 lb. fruit (500 g). Cut the fruit in pieces, removing stones and cores. Blend on slow speed until the purée begins to rise and then switch to fast.

With cooked fruit no liquid is needed, nor with raw juicy fruits.

Purées made with fruit containing very small seeds may need to be strained before use.

VEGETABLES

Soft, watery vegetables like tomatoes can be pulped without added water. Cut the tomatoes in two or three pieces but there is no need to skin them. Straining may be necessary to remove all pips.

Soft cooked or canned vegetables generally require no liquid, but firmer ones need ¼ pt. liquid (150 ml) to 1 lb. of vegetables (500 g).

When the purée is for recipes containing liquid use some of this to help with the blending. Put the liquid in the goblet first, then add some of the vegetables and, when it forms a purée, more can be added.

MEAT

The only raw meats which can be pulped satisfactorily are the very soft ones like liver or fat bacon. First remove any fibre, skin or other tough bits. Cut the meat in small pieces and blend only small amounts at a time. If the meat is put in through the top while the motor is running more can be processed at a time.

Cooked meats should be cut in small pieces and all skin, bone and gristle removed. It can be blended dry in small amounts, (about 4 oz. or 125 g), to give a fine mince or shredded meat; but if a smooth purée is required, some liquid should be added; ¼ pt. liquid (150 ml) to 8 oz. meat (250 g). Only large blenders will process as much as 8 oz. at a time.

FISH

To purée raw fish remove all skin and bone and cut the fish in strips. A large blender will do up to 8 oz. (250 g) at a time.

Cooked fish should be cut in small pieces, or flaked, and all bones and skin removed. It can than be blended dry to shred it but if a smooth purée is required, some liquid should be added; ¼ pt. (150 ml) to 8 oz. fish (250 g).

TO MAKE SMOOTH LIQUIDS

The very early blenders were only used for making liquids, hence the use of the name "liquidiser". It is still one of the most useful jobs the blender will do. A number of recipes are included for drinks, soups, sauces, dressings and fruit juices, see the index.

TO CHOP AND GRATE

The blender does this operation faster than by any other method.

BREADCRUMBS

The blender saves a great deal of time here as well as producing very fine crumbs. In addition, flavouring materials, such as herbs for stuffings, can be blended with the bread bringing about a better distribution of flavours.

The amount of bread which can be blended at a time depends on the capacity of the goblet, the staleness of the bread, and the method of blending. An average amount is $1\frac{1}{2}$ – 2 oz. or 1 – 2 slices. In all cases the bread should be torn or cut into small pieces before blending.

One method of making crumbs is to drop the bread in with the motor running at slow speed and continue adding bread until the blades begin to slow down, or until the goblet is about a third full. This is the better method to use with fresh bread.

The other way is to add a definite amount, generally about $1\frac{1}{2}$ – 2 oz. (40 – 50 g), with the motor off. Then process at slow speed until the crumbs are as fine as required.

Either fresh or stale bread can be used but be sure the blender is dry before you begin. If the bread is very dry and hard it must either be broken up very small before blending or else dropped in while the machine is running, otherwise hard bits may lodge under the blades and prevent them from revolving properly; but keep one hand over the top of the goblet to stop pieces from flying out.

CAKE AND BISCUIT CRUMBS

Break the cake or biscuits into small pieces and put in the goblet with the motor off. Process at slow speed. If hard biscuits are being processed first switch to high speed and then quickly back to slow. This prevents hard bits from lodging under the blades.

Plain crackers and water biscuits crumbs make a good substitute for dried breadcrumbs for coating food for frying.

BUTTERED CRUMBS

Butter the bread before crumbing it.

CHEESE CRUMBS (for toppings and gratins)

Blend a few small pieces of cheese with the bread.

DRIED CRUMBS

Dry the bread slowly in the oven, or use dry crusts for golden crumbs. Break the bread in small pieces and blend using the on/off technique until they are fine.

CHEESE

For dry cheese to sprinkle on food, use a firm cheese; an ideal way of using up dried end pieces. Cut the cheese in 1 inch squares (2 cm), smaller if the cheese is very hard.

With a large blender it is possible to add the cheese with the motor running and continue putting in more until it gets sticky. This method is only suitable with very dry cheese.

I prefer to process up to 2 oz. (50 g) at a time, filling the goblet with the motor off and processing at slow speed.

When the recipe uses liquid and eggs the cheese can be blended with hot or cold liquid and other ingredients, for example, in soups, sauces and many savoury dishes. If the recipe includes breadcrumbs the cheese may be blended while making the crumbs.

When using soft and processed cheese it is better to blend them with liquid.

CHOCOLATE

Break it in small pieces and put it in the goblet with the motor running at slow speed.

When it is being used in sauces and puddings, blend the chocolate with some of the warm liquid in the recipe. This avoids the troublesome and messy business of melting chocolate over hot water in the conventional way.

HERBS

Herbs which have been washed and well-drained can be chopped fairly successfully by adding them through the top with the motor running, using about a handful of herbs for a large goblet. More satisfactory with most blenders is to add about 2 tablespoons of water and then strain the herbs after chopping.

Herbs for a sauce or soup can be blended with some of the liquid and then added to the main mixture. Be careful not to over-blend or the juice from green herbs will make the whole sauce green.

For stuffings chop green herbs with the bread but be sure they are not wet or the bread will go soggy.

Horseradish can be chopped dry, adding small pieces through the top with the motor running; or blend it with some of the liquid in the sauce, or with thick cream.

LEMON OR ORANGE RIND

In all cases pare the rind very thinly in strips. It can be chopped dry or mixed with sugar in the proportions of 2 tablespoons of sugar to 1 orange or lemon. Use the on/off technique until the rind is finely chopped.

If there are breadcrumbs in the recipe, blend strips of peel with the bread as it is crumbed.

If there is liquid in the recipe, or egg, the peel may be blended with these.

NUTS

Nuts can be chopped, or ground to a fine powder. This not only enables a variety of ground nuts to be used in cooking, (instead of just commercial ground almonds), but makes it much simpler to prepare the delicious continental biscuits and nut gâteaux.

Pick over the shelled nuts to make sure no bits of shell are included; 3 – 4 oz. (100 g) can usually be processed at a time in a large goblet. Use either the on/off technique at slow speed until the nuts are chopped as finely as required; or drop the nuts through the top with the motor running at slow speed, keeping the top covered with one hand.

When finely ground oily nuts like almonds are being processed it helps to prevent excessive oiling if a little cold water or lemon juice is added.

PEEL, CANDIED

Cut it in 1 inch (2 cm) pieces and fill through the top with the motor running. Process 3 – 4 oz. at a time (100 g.)

PRALINE AND NUT TOFFEE

It is useful to be able to powder these for garnishing and flavouring cakes, ices and puddings. Blend only a small amount at a time, first breaking it into fairly small pieces. Blend on slow speed.

SUET

Cut the suet in pieces, removing as much membrane as possible. Blend it with flour, about half a goblet at a time. It chops very quickly and only a second, or on/off, is usually sufficient.

SUGAR

Coarse granulated sugar can be turned into fine caster or icing sugar and lumpy icing sugar can be made smooth. If you use much caster sugar this can make quite a cost saving. Put in enough sugar to cover the blender blades, but do not fill the goblet more than a quarter. It takes about 20 seconds to make caster sugar. If icing sugar is made this way it will not be as white as commercial icing sugar and is better used in tinted icings.

Coloured sugars for decorating cakes and puddings can be made by putting granulated sugar in the blender with a few drops of colouring and blending just to mix.

VEGETABLES

The blender will chop or grate vegetables faster than any other machine. Prepare them in the usual way and cut them into 1 inch (2 cm) pieces. With some very large blenders this is not necessary and whole vegetables can be processed satisfactorily.

When only small amounts are being processed, feed them into the goblet with the motor running at fast speed and chop until as fine as required.

For large amounts, cover the vegetables with cold water and blend for about 5 seconds or less. Drain on a sieve, reserving the liquid if stock is required.

For salads, sauces and spreads the vegetables may be chopped with any dressing, sauce or other liquid ingredients. If mixed vegetables are used and some are required finely chopped and others left coarser, process the fine ones first and then add the others just long enough to chop as required.

If you keep a supply of frozen, sliced vegetables like mushrooms and green peppers, these can be chopped while still frozen, without using any liquid.

USING GELATINE AND JELLIES

Provided the recipe has as much as ¼ pint (150 ml) of liquid in it, the gelatine can be dissolved in the blender, thus cutting out the usual separate mixing; but less than this is not satisfactory as the undissolved gelatine is just flung against the sides of the goblet and sticks there. Put the hot liquid in the goblet, sprinkle in the gelatine, and blend for a few seconds before adding the rest of the ingredients. If these have been chilled the final jelly will set very quickly. Alternatively, some crushed ice can be processed with the other ingredients but allow for the bulk of this by reducing the amount of other liquid; $\frac{1}{2}$ pint (250 ml) of crushed ice is equal to about half that quantity of water. Remember, too, that the ice has no flavour and will dilute that in the jelly.

Packet jellies can be dissolved quickly by putting half the necessary hot water in the blender, adding the broken jelly and blending for the minimum time needed. If the remaining liquid is ice-cold, the jelly will set very quickly.

USING INSTANT AND PACKET MIXES

Provided the final mixture will be a soft one, the blender can be used to simplify and speed up the mixing process. Put the required amount of liquid in the goblet, add the contents of the packet, eggs if required, and blend thoroughly.

WHISKING EGGS

Break them into the goblet and process at full speed for a few seconds. Do this for scrambled eggs and omelets too. It takes less time to rinse out the blender than to wash a basin and beater.

Egg yolks can be whisked with 1 tablespoon of water per yolk, or use milk or stock as the liquid.

Egg whites can be whisked to mix them but the blender will not beat them properly for meringues and similar uses.

CRUSHING ICE

When ice is required for cooling drinks and cold sweets it is usually more satisfactory to crush it first, though some manufacturers of large blenders recommend adding whole ice cubes.

To crush ice cubes wrap them in a clean cloth and bang with a wooden rolling pin. To break each cube into 3 or 4 pieces is sufficiently small. If you have one of the ice trays which makes very small cubes or balls of ice, these require no crushing.

When adding ice to a recipe remember that it dilutes the flavour, so allow for this. Adding $\frac{1}{2}$ pint (250 ml) of crushed ice is equivalent to adding about $\frac{1}{4}$ pint (150 ml) of water, by the time it has melted.

Chapter Four

PÂTÉS AND SPREADS

PÂTÉS OR TERRINES

Those made with raw liver can be blended before cooking but other meats should be cooked first. When fat bacon is included this can be blended raw provided it is cut small and added to a sauce or liquid before blending.

If cooked ingredients are blended while they are still hot or warm, they produce a thinner mixture which is easier to remove from the goblet. Butter, or other fat added, should be melted and, when the pâté is cold, this will set and give a firm result.

I have included a number of different recipes, some giving a soft spreadable texture, others are firmer for slicing.

SPREADS

Although most recipes for spreads can be blended satisfactorily, some are so thick when finished that they are difficult to scrape out of the goblet without a lot of waste round the blades. If ingredients are blended hot or warm they will be softer and easier to tip out, and if the mixture includes melted butter or margarine they will be quite firm when cold.

When cooked meats or poultry are being used it is often better if these are blended first by themselves and then the other ingredients added or blended separately and mixed in later.

DIPS

Many recipes for spreads can be turned into dips by replacing the butter or margarine in the recipe by cream, yogurt, mayonnaise or salad dressing, or by a soft cheese.

BEEF PÂTÉ OR SPREAD

This is a modern version of the old English potted beef, made for sandwich spreads. After cooking, the meat was pounded in a mortar or rubbed through a sieve, laborious operations, today replaced by the blender. The mixture sets firmly enough to be turned out as a loaf and sliced, but it is also spreadable.

COOKING TIME: 2½ – 3 hrs. TEMPERATURE: E.350°F (180°C) G.4. QUANTITIES for 8 or more.

1 lb stewing steak (500 g): ¼ pt stock (150 ml): Pinch of ground cloves: ¼ tsp ground mace: ½ tsp salt: Pinch of pepper: 1 small bay leaf

Trim off surplus fat from the meat and cut the meat in ½ inch (1 cm) cubes. Put it in a casserole with the other ingredients. Cover and cook slowly until the meat is quite tender. Remove the bay leaf. Strain and, if necessary, make the liquid up to ¼ pt (150 ml) with stock.

2 oz butter or margarine (50 g): 2 Tbs red wine

Melt the fat and blend with the meat, stock, and wine, doing this while the meat and stock are still hot and in several lots, depending on the capacity of the blender. It is a fairly thick mixture and most blenders will only take about a quarter of this at a time. When the mixture is all smooth and finally mixed together, turn into a dish, cool quickly, cover and store in the refrigerator until required.

CHEESE AND WALNUT SPREAD

Suitable for a sandwich spread or use on toast in the same way as Welsh Rarebit. It is very good indeed when made with blue cheese but the colour of it might put some people off. The alternative is to make it with strong cheddar or to blend in parsley or paprika pepper to mask the colour.

4 oz blue or other cheese (125 g): Few grains cayenne pepper: 2 oz melted butter or margarine (50 g): 3 Tbs mayonnaise

Have the cheese at room temperature and cut it in pieces. Blend all the ingredients together at slow speed until smooth.

1 oz shelled walnuts (25 g)

Add to the cheese mixture and blend just to chop the nuts finely. Put in a covered dish and store in the refrigerator when it will become quite firm.

CHICKEN LIVER SPREAD

COOKING TIME: 15 mins.
1 small onions: 1 Tbs oil

Peel the onion and chop it dry in the blender at slow speed. Heat the oil in a frying pan and cook the onion in it until it begins to brown. Tip out on to a saucer.

8 oz chicken livers (250 g): 1 Tbs oil

Remove any skin and fat from the livers. Add the oil to the frying pan and fry the livers gently for about 10 minutes or until they are cooked.

1 hard boiled egg: 2 Tbs lemon juice: 6 Tbs oil: Salt and pepper
Shell the egg and cut it up roughly. Put all the ingredients, including the onion and liver, in the goblet, processing it smooth in one or two lots depending on the capacity of the goblet. Scrape down and add more oil if necessary. Put in a small covered dish and store in the refrigerator. Serve with toast or as a sandwich spread

CHICKEN LIVER PÂTÉ

This soft, spreadable pâté requires no oven cooking, being merely fried and blended.

COOKING TIME: 8 – 10 mins. QUANTITIES for 8 or more
1 lb chicken livers (500 g)

Wash the livers, dry on kitchen paper and remove any skin or stringy bits.

1 small onion

Skin, and either slice finely or blend to chop small.

2 oz butter (50 g)

Heat some of the butter and fry the liver quickly in it for 3–4 minutes. Remove. Heat enough more butter to fry the onion until tender. Add any remaining butter and allow it to melt. Put aside to cool a little, but do not allow the ingredients to become cold or blending will be more difficult.

½ tsp salt: Pinch cayenne pepper: Pinch powdered marjoram: Pinch ground mace: 3 or more Tbs marsala or sherry

Put in the goblet with the liver and onions and blend until smooth.

Pack into a dish and cool quickly. Store in the refrigerator or freezer.

CHICKEN LIVER TERRINE

This makes a terrine firm enough to slice but also suitable for spreading. Raw bacon is blended with the other ingredients giving a good mixture of flavours.

COOKING TIME: 1½ hrs. TEMPERATURE E. 350°F (180°C) G.4. QUANTITIES for 8 or more

8 oz chicken livers (250 g): 8 oz pig's liver (250 g)

Remove any skin and tubes and cut the liver in strips. Rinse it in cold water and drain. Blend it to a pulp in two or more lots depending on the capacity of the blender. Tip into a mixing bowl.

4 oz fat bacon (125 g)

Remove rinds and cut in small pieces.

1 oz flour (25 g): Pinch dried garlic: ¼ pt milk (150 ml): 4 Tbs cream or stock: 2 Tbs sherry or brandy: 2 eggs: 1 tsp salt: Pinch of pepper

Put all in the goblet, add the bacon and blend to mix well and chop the bacon finely. Add to the liver, mix well and pour into an oiled baking tin or dish, capacity about 2 pints (1 l). Cover with a lid and stand the dish in a pan of hot water and bake. Remove from the water, cool for a while and then place a weight on top and leave until quite cold before storing in the refrigerator or freezer.

COTTAGE CHEESE AND HORSERADISH
SPREAD OR DIP

8 oz cottage cheese (250 g): ¼ tsp salt: 2 – 3 Tbs bottled horse-radish sauce: 2 oz melted butter (50 g) or 3 – 4 Tbs cream

For a spread use the melted butter, and the cream for a dip. Blend the ingredients in one or more lots depending on the capacity of the blender. The cheese should be at room temperature.

2 – 3 sprigs of parsley

Break up and add to the last lot being blended and process just enough to chop the parsley but not to make the whole mixture green.

CRAB SANDWICH SPREAD

4 oz crab meat (125): 1 tsp capers: 1 slice of green pepper; ½ tsp Worcester sauce: ½ Tbs vinegar: 1 oz melted butter or margarine (25 g): ½ tsp dry mustard: Pinch of pepper: ¼ tsp salt

Put all in the goblet and blend with an on/off action until the mixture is well combined and the pepper chopped finely. Store in a covered container in the refrigerator.

EGG AND ONION SPREAD

2 oz onion (50 g): 2 Tbs oil: ½ tsp salt: Pinch of pepper

Cut the onion in pieces and blend with the oil and seasonings to chop it finely.

4 hard-boiled eggs

Shell and cut in quarters. Add to the onions and blend just to chop the eggs. Store in a covered container in the refrigerator. The mixture is suitable for a spread, for hors d'œuvre, or open sandwiches.

FISH PÂTÉ OR SPREAD

8 oz cooked white fish (250 g): 3 Tbs lemon juice: Pepper and paprika pepper: 2 tps anchovy essence or 3 – 4 anchovy fillets: 4 oz melted butter or margarine (125 g)

For easy mixing it is better to make this while the fish is still warm or at room temperature. Carefully remove any skin or bone and put the fish and other ingredients in the blender. Blend until creamy. Store in the refrigerator in a covered container. Serve with toast as a pâté, or use for a spread for sandwiches or canapés.

KIPPER PÂTÉ OR SPREAD

1½ lb kippers (750 g): 8 oz butter or margarine (250 g)

Wash the kippers, put them in a jug and cover with boiling water. Set aside for 10 minutes. Drain, remove all bones and skin and put them in the blender goblet, or put half in the goblet and blend the rest afterwards. Melt the butter or margarine and add half to half the fish. Blend together until smooth. Put in a bowl.

1 tsp anchovy essence: Pepper: Lemon juice

Add seasoning to taste and pack the mixture into small containers. Cover and store in the refrigerator. Serve with toast as a pâté, or as a sandwich filling.

LIVER SAUSAGE SPREAD

4 oz soft liver sausage (125 g): 1 tsp French mustard: 4 Tbs mayonnaise: 1 oz melted bacon fat or lard (25 g)

Put in the goblet and blend until smooth.

2 rashers crisply fried bacon, cut up: 2 small gherkins, cut up

Add to the liver and mix just enough to chop bacon and gherkins. When stored in the refrigerator the spread becomes firmer. Should the mixture seem too stiff during blending, add more mayonnaise.

MIXED LIVER TERRINE

This one is cooked in a terrine lined with bacon and is firm enough for slicing.

COOKING TIME: 1½ hrs. TEMPERATURE: E. 350°F (180°C) G.4.
QUANTITIES for 8 or more

8 thin rashers streaky bacon

Remove the rinds and use the bacon to line a 2 lb (1 kg) loaf tin or similar baking dish such as a 2 pint (1 l) pie-dish.

4 oz chicken livers (125 g): 4 oz pig's liver (125 g): 1 lb calf's or lamb's liver (500 g)

Remove any skin and tubes from the liver. Cut it in strips and rinse in cold water.

4 Tbs double cream: 1 egg: 1 clove fresh garlic or ¼ tsp dried: 1 Tbs lemon juice: 2 Tbs brandy: Salt and pepper

Blend these together until the liver is pulped, doing it in one or more lots depending on the size of the blender. If done in several lots, tip each into a bowl as it is finished and then mix all together before putting into the bacon-lined dish. Stand this in a baking tin of hot water. Cover the terrine and bake. Remove from the water and allow to cool for a while, then put a weight on top and leave until quite cold before storing in the refrigerator or freezer.

PIGS'S LIVER TERRINE

This is a soft, rich terrine containing lard. When chilled, it can be sliced, but is more suitable for serving with a spoon and is very good for spreading.

COOKING TIME: 1 – 1½ hrs. TEMPERATURE: E. 375°F (190°C) G.5. QUANTITIES for a 1½ pt (1 l) dish

8 oz pig's liver (250 g): 4 oz lard (125 g)

Remove any skin and tubes from the liver. Cut it in small pieces, rinse in cold water and drain. Melt or soften the lard if it is very cold and hard. Blend liver and lard together at slow speed. Do this in one or two lots depending on the size of the blender. Tip into a mixing bowl.

1½ Tbs flour: 1 egg: ½ pt milk (250 ml): 1 tsp salt: Pinch pepper: 2 Tbs sherry: 1 slice of onion

Blend all together until smooth, add to the liver and mix well. Pour into the well-greased dish. Stand this in a pan of hot water and bake, uncovered, until it is set. Leave to become quite cold before storing in the refrigerator or freezer.

POTTED DUCK

A good way of using up some of the duck dripping and the small pieces of meat left on a carcass. Using all dripping for the fat makes a soft spread: for a firmer one, use some butter or firm margarine.

QUANTITIES for 8 oz (250 g)

4 oz cooked duck meat (125 g): 2 oz duck dripping or use half softened butter or margarine and half dripping (50 g); 1 Tbs brandy, marsala or dry sherry: Pinch of ground cloves: ¼ tsp salt: 1 tsp lemon juice: 4–5 Tbs duck stock or gravy

Put all ingredients in the goblet and blend to a smooth paste adding as much stock or gravy as required for easy blending. Put in a covered container and store in the refrigerator. Serve with toast as an hors d'œuvre, or use for sandwiches.

POTTED TONGUE

QUANTITIES for 6 oz spread (150 g)

*2 Tbs mayonnaise or salad cream: 2 Tbs red wine or stock: 4 oz
diced cooked tongue (125 g): 1 oz melted butter (25 g): ¼ tsp
ground mace: Pinch ground cloves: Few grains cayenne pepper*

Put in the goblet in that order and blend until smooth. Put in a
covered container and store in the refrigerator. Use as a sandwich
filling.

ROLLMOP SPREAD OR DIP

*¼ pt double cream (150 ml): 3 oz melted butter or margarine
(75 g): 1 onion or use that in the rollmops: 2 rollmops*

Unfasten the rollmops and remove the tails. Cut the fish in strips.
If fresh onion is used, peel and cut in pieces. Put all ingredients
in the goblet and blend on slow speed until a vortex forms,
then faster until the mixture is smooth. Store in the refrigerator
until required.

To make this soft enough for a dip, added more cream or
some mayonnaise or salad cream.

SALMON AND EGG SPREAD

*2 hard boiled eggs: 2 Tbs mayonnaise: 3½ – 4 oz canned salmon,
including oil and bones (100 g): 2 strips green pepper*

Put all ingredients in the goblet and blend until smooth. The egg
whites can be reserved for a garnish if the spread is being used for
an open sandwich, otherwise add the whites and blend just
enough to chop them.

SARDINE AND CHEESE PÂTÉ OR SPREAD

3 – 4 oz can sardines (125 g)

Put the sardines in the blender goblet with the oil in the can and
blend smooth: Sometimes there is very little oil and it may be
necessary to add a little extra to help the blending.

4 oz melted butter or margarine (125 g): 1 slice of onion: 2 Tbs lemon juice: 2 oz cheese cut in pieces (50 g): ¼ tsp paprika pepper: Salt and pepper

Add to the fish and blend until smooth. The mixture should be soft and easy to remove from the goblet. After several hours, or overnight, in the refrigerator it is firm enough to turn out and slice, but is still spreadable.

SARDINE AND OLIVE SANDWICH FILLING

3 Tbs mayonnaise: 1 × 4½ oz can of sardines in oil (125 g): 1 Tbs lemon juice: 4 stuffed olives: Pinch of garlic salt: Pinch of pepper: 2 oz melted butter or margarine (50 g)

Put all in the goblet, including the sardine oil. Blend, turning on/off and scraping down as necessary. Put in a dish with a lid and store in the refrigerator. Sitr before using.

SMOKED COD'S ROE SPREAD

¼ pt olive oil (150 ml): Pinch of cayenne pepper: 2 Tbs lemon juice: ½ tsp dry mustard: 8 oz smoked cod's roe (250 g)

Remove any hard skin from the outside and put the roe and other ingredients in the goblet. Blend, on/off at low speed, just to mix well, adding more oil if the mixture is too stiff for easy blending. Store in the refrigerator in a covered dish.

Alternative. To make a spread which will be firm when cold, use 4 oz (125 g) of melted butter or margarine in place of the oil.

SMOKED MACKEREL OR BUCKLING PÂTÉ OR SPREAD

6 oz fillets of smoked mackerel or buckling (150 g) or about ¾ lb of whole fish (375 g)

Remove all skin and bone from the fish. If there are roes, use them as well. Break the fish in small pieces and set aside.

4 Tbs single cream: 4 oz cream cheese at room temperature (125 g)

Put in the goblet and blend smooth.

2 Tbs white wine: 1 Tbs lemon juice: A few chives: ¼ tsp paprika pepper: Salt and pepper

Add to the goblet and blend to chop the chives.

2 oz melted butter or margarine (50 g) or 4 Tbs oil

Add to the goblet with some of the fish. Blend smooth. Add the remaining fish and some more cream if necessary. With some goblets it may be necessary to do the fish blending in two lots. Before adding any fish, tip out half the mixture in the goblet, add half the fish and blend. Tip out and do the other half of the ingredients.

Store the mixture in a covered dish in the refrigerator. For hors d'œuvre serve the pâté with toast.

SPICED LIVER PÂTÉ OR SPREAD

This strongly flavoured pâté requires no oven cooking, ingredients being fried and then blended. The texture is soft and spreadable.

COOKING TIME: 5 – 10 mins. QUANTITIES for 8 or more

8 oz pig's or calf's liver (250 g)

Remove any skin and tubes and cut in small pieces. Rinse in cold water and drain.

1 oz butter or margarine (25 g): 2 sprigs parsley: 8 oz mild fat bacon (250 g): Pinch pepper: 1 tsp mixed spice

Remove rinds and cut bacon in pieces. Melt the fat and fry the bacon in it for a few minutes. Add the liver and the other ingredients and fry slowly until the liver is just cooked. Avoid overcooking as this spoils the texture of the pâté.

2 anchovy fillets or 1 tsp anchovy essence: ¼ pt red wine (150 ml)

Put in the blender with the fried ingredients and any juices in the pan. Do this in one or more lots depending on the size of the blender. Blend until smooth. Tip into a dish and leave until quite cold before storing in the refrigerator.

TUNA SPREAD

QUANTITIES for 8 oz (250 g)

3 oz Dutch or Cheddar cheese, cut up (75 g)

29

Blend the cheese on slow speed to grate it coarsely. Tip into a small bowl.

> *3 oz canned tuna with bones and oil (75 g): 1 oz melted butter or margarine (25 g): 2 Tbs cream: Salt and pepper: 2 pickled walnuts, cut in half*

Put all in the goblet making sure there are no bits of shell in the walnuts. Blend smooth and add to the cheese. Mix well. If more liquid seems to be needed for smooth blending, add more cream or some of the liquid from the pickled walnuts. Put in a covered dish in the refrigerator.

Chapter Five

SOUPS – HOT AND COLD

With most soups a blender can be a help at some stage of the making and with many it will make the preparation one-stage only. It is specially useful where a creamy mixture is important, the blender giving a texture equal to that only obtained by long and laborious methods followed by an older generation of cooks.

The cooking of vegetable soups is speeded up and a better flavour obtained if the vegetables are blended raw; but, unless they are tender ones, the texture is not as smooth as when blending takes place after cooking. You can always give a final quick blend to this kind of soup just before serving it.

Canned vegetables are excellent for quick soups and sometimes give a better flavour than the home-cooked ones. Some very delicate soups are obtained in this way, for example, Corn Soup or Carrot Soup.

Left-over cooked vegetables make excellent cream soups, especially spinach, cauliflower and carrot, or use a mixture of vegetables.

When tomatoes, or celery and other fibrous vegetables are used, the soup may need straining after blending if an absolutely smooth texture is required.

With pulse soups the cooking time can be reduced by about half if the peas or lentils are either blended raw with a little of the water or stock, or blended dry to a fine powder, before making the soup.

Most goblets are heat resistant but it is a good idea, nevertheless, to warm the goblet first, specially if the soup will be served straight from the goblet. Only two thirds fill the goblet and remember to keep a hand on the lid while switching on.

One of the joys of blender soups is that they don't need to have starchy thickenings added to produce a smooth texture. If, however, your family likes very thick soups, then flour, cornflour or potato can be blended with the other ingredients, or potato powder can be blended in at the end. To thicken with egg yolk and cream, blend these with a little of the hot soup, add to the rest, stir and serve.

When milk or cream is added, do it at the end and avoid over-blending or the soup may curdle.

FIVE METHODS OF MAKING BLENDER VEGETABLE SOUPS

1. Blend raw, young vegetables with water or stock and flavourings, then cook.
2. Blend raw vegetables to chop them coarsely, sweat them in a little butter or margarine in the usual way for a vegetable soup; then blend them with stock or milk, heat and season.
3. Blend cooked or canned vegetables with stock, milk, cream and flavourings; heat, or use as a cold soup.
4. Blend raw vegetables with cold stock, or milk and cream. Add herbs and other flavourings and use for cold soups.
5. Blend canned soups with appropriate canned or cooked meat, poultry or fish, and stock or milk. Heat and season.

ASPARAGUS SOUP

COOKING TIME: 3 – 4 mins. QUANTITIES for 4 – 6

1 lb can of asparagus (500 g): Salt and pepper: ½ – ¾ pt milk (250 – 300 ml): Cream or evaporated milk

Empty the asparagus and its liquid into the blender goblet and mix until smooth. Put in a pan with some of the milk and heat gently. Add more milk to give the consistency desired. Season to taste and add a little cream or milk before serving. No thickening is necessary.

CARROT SOUP

This is a lovely orange-coloured soup with a delicate flavour. It is, however, necessary to use a really well-flavoured stock or the canned consommé, otherwise the soup will be disappointing.

COOKING TIME: 5 mins. QUANTITIES for 3 – 4

12 oz cooked or canned carrots, drained weight (375 g): 10½ oz can of concentrated consommé or good stock (300 ml)

Strain the carrots and use the carrot stock to dilute the consommé, using half a can of carrot stock. Put the carrots in the goblet with enough of the stock to moisten. Blend smooth and tip into a pan. Add remaining stock to give the consistency desired. Heat gently.

Salt: Pinch of cayenne: A little cream

Season to taste and add a little cream just before serving. There should be no need to thicken this soup.

CAULIFLOWER SOUP

This can be made with either left-over or freshly cooked cauliflower. It makes a smooth, thin creamy soup but, if a thick soup is preferred, a tablespoon of cornflour or potato flour can be blended with the other ingredients, or include some left-over white sauce.

COOKING TIME: a few mins. QUANTITIES for 4

8 oz cooked cauliflower (250 g): 1 chicken cube or ½ pt chicken stock (250 ml): ½ pt milk (250 ml): 1 oz diced cheese (25 g): Pinch of mace or nutmeg: Salt and pepper: Cream, optional

Put half the cauliflower in the goblet with the milk, cheese, chicken cube and seasonings. Blend for 30 seconds. Add the rest of the cauliflower and blend for another 30 seconds, or until quite smooth. Tip into a saucepan. Use ½ pt (250 ml) of cold water to rinse out the goblet, or use chicken stock. Add to the soup, heat until boiling and taste for seasoning. Add the cream if used, and serve garnished with a little paprika pepper or chopped green herbs.

CELERY SOUP

COOKING TIME: 30 – 45 mins. QUANTITIES for 4 – 6

8 sticks celery: 2 rashers bacon: 1½ pt white stock (1 l): 1 oz butter or margarine (25 g): Salt: Pinch of mace or nutmeg: 1 tsp sugar

Wash the celery and slice it. Remove rinds and cut the bacon in pieces. Put all ingredients in a pan and simmer until the celery is tender. Cool a little and then blend in two or more lots, for 1 minute. Rinse the pan and strain the soup back in, to remove any unblended fibres. Re-heat.

¼ pt cream or evaporated milk (150 ml)

Add to the soup, taste for seasoning and serve hot.

Alternative. If a thicker soup is preferred, blend a tablespoon of cornflour or potato flour with the soup. If cornflour is used, boil for 2 – 3 minutes before adding the cream.

CHEESE AND WATERCRESS SOUP

COOKING TIME: 10 – 15 mins. QUANTITIES for 3 – 4

1 pt hot milk (500 ml): 1 tsp cornflour: ½ tsp dry mustard: 1 oz butter or margarine (25 g): 2 oz cheese (50 g): Salt and pepper

Cut the cheese in pieces and put all ingredients in the goblet. Blend until smooth. Tip back into the pan and stir until it boils. Simmer for 2–3 minutes.

1 oz watercress (25 g)

Wash the cress and cut up roughly. Put it in the goblet with enough soup to cover, and blend just to chop it. Return to the main soup, mix and taste for seasoning.

CHICKEN SOUP

This soup is the kind which takes a long time to make using conventional methods but is quickly made when the method is adapted for the blender. It is a smooth, creamy soup with an excellent flavour; and makes use of a chicken carcass and remains of the meat.

COOKING TIME: ½ hr. for the stock; a few mins. for the soup
QUANTITIES for 4 – 6

1 chicken carcass

Use the pressure cooker to make stock with the carcass. Strain.

8 oz cooked chicken meat (250 g): 2 Tbs flour: 1½ pt chicken stock (750 ml)

Cut the chicken meat in pieces and blend all together until smooth, about 1 minute. Pour into a pan, heat to boiling, stirring occasionally. Simmer for 2 – 3 minutes. Keep hot until ready to serve.

1 egg yolk: 4 Tbs cream or evaporated milk

Mix and add to the soup.

Salt and pepper: Lemon juice: A little white wine: Tarragon leaves, optional

Season the soup and, if the tarragon is used, blend it with a little stock or soup, just to chop finely. Add to the soup and serve.

CORN SOUP

COOKING TIME: 10 – 20 mins. QUANTITIES for 4

12 oz cooked or canned sweet corn kernels or niblets (375 g): ½ pt water (250 ml): 1 thick slice of onion

Put in the goblet and blend until smooth. If you want to be quite sure there are no unblended bits left, strain it into the pan.

¾ pt milk (400 ml)

Add to the pan and bring to the boil, stirring frequently. Simmer over a gentle heat for 10 minutes, or in a double boiler for 20 minutes.

Salt and pepper: 1 oz butter (25 g)

Season to taste and add the butter. Stir until it melts and serve the soup hot garnished with

Paprika pepper

CUCUMBER SOUP

COOKING TIME: 15 mins. QUANTITIES for 6

1 lb cucumber (½ kg or 1 large): 1 small onion: 2 pt chicken stock (1 l)

Peel the cucumber and cut it in cubes. Skin and cut the onion in pieces. Blend these smooth with a little of the stock. Put in a pan with the remaining stock and simmer until the onion tastes cooked.

2 egg yolks: ¼ pt yogurt or soured cream (150 ml): Salt and pepper: Paprika pepper to garnish

Put egg yolks and yogurt or cream in the goblet with a little of the soup, blend again and return to the pan. Stir and heat until it thickens slightly but do not boil. Season to taste and serve with a sprinkling of paprika pepper as a garnish.

SOUPE FLAMANDE OR PURÉE OF BRUSSELS SPROUTS

COOKING TIME: ½ hr. QUANTITIES for 4 – 6

1 lb fresh or frozen Brussels sprouts (500 g)

Wash and trim the fresh sprouts. Part-boil either kind and drain.

3 oz butter (75 g)

Melt the butter and stew the sprouts in it until the butter is almost absorbed.

1 pt white stock (½ l): 2 medium potatoes

Peel and quarter the potatoes and add them to the pan with the stock. Simmer for about 20 minutes or until the vegetables are tender. Put the soup in the blender in two or more lots and mix smooth. Tip back into the pan.

½ pt milk (250 ml): Salt and pepper

Swill out the blender goblet with the milk and add it to the soup. Re-heat and season to taste. Add more milk or cream if a thinner soup is required. Serve hot.

PORTUGUESE ALMOND SOUP

This is a smooth, white, creamy soup and no thickening is required. It has a delicate flavour which is spoiled by using chicken cubes instead of home-made chicken or veal stock.

COOKING TIME: 15 mins. QUANTITIES for 4

4 oz blanched almonds (125 g): 1 slice of onion: 1 stalk of celery cut in pieces: 1 pt white stock (½ l)

Blend the almonds, celery and onion with stock to cover, blending about 1 minute, or until smooth. Pour into a pan and add the rest of the stock. Bring to the boil and simmer for 15 minutes.

Salt and pepper: ¼ pt cream or evaporated milk (150 ml)

Season to taste and add the cream or milk. Make sure it is hot before serving. Garnish with

Chopped red pepper or paprika pepper

POTATO AND ONION SOUP

COOKING TIME: ¾ – 1 hr. QUANTITIES for 6 or more

2 medium onions: 1 lb potatoes (500 g): 1 oz butter or margarine (25 g)

Peel the onions and potatoes. Slice the potatoes and blend the onions dry to chop them coarsely, or slice them too. Melt the fat in a saucepan and stew the vegetables in it for about 10 minutes, but not allowing them to brown.

1½ pt white stock (750 ml)

Add to the vegetables, bring to the boil and simmer gently until the vegetables are cooked, about 30 – 40 minutes.

½ pt cold milk (250 ml)

Put some of the milk in the goblet and add some of the soup. Blend smooth. Repeat until all except a couple of tablespoons of the milk is left. Re-heat the soup.

Salt and pepper: A knob of butter: 2 – 3 sprigs of parsley

Season the soup and add the butter. Blend the parsley with the 2 Tbs of milk until it is finely chopped. Add to the soup and serve.

TUNA BISQUE

This is a good way of using canned tuna and makes a substantial soup for a first course in a light meal.

COOKING TIME: a few minutes. QUANTITIES for 4

2 slices of onion: ½ pt liquid (250 ml) using milk plus liquid from the fish: 1 slice of green pepper or a stalk of celery: 1 oz butter or margarine (25 g)

Put all in the goblet and blend smooth, about 1 minute. Pour into a pan and bring to the boil. Boil for 2 – 3 minutes.

7 oz can of tuna (198 g): ¼ pt tomato juice (150 ml): ¼ pt white stock (150 ml)

Blend together until smooth, about 1 minute. Add to the other liquid and bring to the boil. Remove from the heat, season to taste, and serve. Garnish with

Chopped parsley or other green herbs such as fennel or dill

COLD SOUPS
BORTSCH

QUANTITIES for 4

10½ oz can concentrated consommé (250 ml): 8 oz cooked beetroot (250 g): 2 Tbs evaporated milk: Salt and pepper: 3 Tbs lemon juice: 1 slice of onion

If the beetroots are large cut them in pieces, first having removed the skins. Put all the ingredients in the blender goblet with half a can of water. Blend until smooth. Chill in the refrigerator.

Green herbs or evaporated milk

Serve garnished with chopped green herbs or a swirl of evaporated milk.

Alternative. If freshly cooked beets are not available, use the small whole bottled pickled beets, draining and rinsing them before use. Taste before deciding to add the lemon juice.

ICED CUCUMBER SOUP

QUANTITIES for 4

1 large or 2 small cucumbers: ½ small onion: 2 Tbs lemon juice: 2 mint leaves

Peel and cut up the cucumber and onion. Put in the goblet with the lemon and mint and blend until smooth.

½ pt canned consommé (250 ml): Salt and pepper: Few prawns or shrimps to garnish

Add the consommé and season to taste. Put in individual dishes or in a large bowl or tureen and refrigerate. Serve with the fish as a garnish.

GASPACHO

A Spanish cold soup of which there are many different regional recipes.

QUANTITIES for 8

1½ pt canned tomato juice (750 ml): 1 lb cucumber (½ kg or 1 large): Sugar, salt and pepper to taste: 2 Tbs olive oil: Pinch dried garlic: 4 Tbs wine vinegar: 2 Tbs red wine

Peel the cucumber and cut it in small pieces. Blend it smooth with a little of the tomato juice. Pour in a bowl and add the other ingredients. Cover and chill.

Parsley

Blend dry and use to garnish the soup.

CREAM OF PEA SOUP

COOKING TIME: 5 – 10 mins. QUANTITIES for 4 – 6

8 oz fresh or frozen peas (250 g): 1 pt good chicken stock (½ l)

Boil the peas in a little salted water. Drain, keeping the liquid. Blend peas to a pulp with ¼ pt (150 ml) of the cooking liquid and some of the stock. The remaining cooking liquid may be used to make up the quantity of stock.

2 – 3 sprigs mint

Add the mint leaves to the goblet and blend to chop. Tip into a pan. Add the rest of the stock, bring to the boil and simmer for a few minutes.

1 egg yolk: ¼ pt double cream (150 ml): Salt and pepper: Sugar to taste

Mix egg yolk, cream and seasonings either in the blender or in a small basin with a little of the soup. Add to the main soup, mix well and taste for seasoning. Cool quickly and then store in the refrigerator until required. If the stock has been a good one this will set on cooling. To break up, whisk lightly or put in the blender for a second.

Diced crisp bacon

Use as a garnish. Grill or fry the bacon before chopping it.

ICED SWEET PEPPER SOUP

QUANTITIES for 6 – 8

14 oz can red peppers or pimentos (400 g): 2 pts canned tomato juice (1 l)

Drain the pimentos and remove any seeds. Blend them smooth with some of the tomato juice. Tip out and mix with remaining juice.

Salt and pepper: Garlic salt or fresh garlic juice

Season the soup to taste and chill thoroughly. If fresh garlic is used for flavouring, blend a little with the pimentos.

Parsley or other green herbs

Blend dry to chop them and use as a garnish for the soup.

VICHYSSOISE

COOKING TIME: 45 mins. QUANTITIES for 4 – 6

4 leeks: 2 oz butter (50 g)

Trim the leeks, discarding the green parts. Cut in half and wash very carefully. Cut across in pieces and blend coarsely. Melt the butter in a saucepan and stew the leeks slowly in it until the butter is absorbed but the leeks are not browned.

3 small, old potatoes

Peel and cut in small pieces. Add to the leeks with water barely to cover the vegetables. Simmer for 15 minutes.

1 pt chicken stock (½ l): Salt and pepper

Add to the pan and simmer until the vegetables are tender. Put in the blender goblet and mix until smooth. Cool and then refrigerate.

¼ pt double cream (150 ml): Chives or parsley

When ready to serve the soup, add the cream, check for seasoning and serve garnished with chopped herbs.

Alternative. This soup is also very good served hot. Add the cream and heat, without boiling.

Chapter Six

SAUCES – HOT, COLD, SWEET – STUFFINGS

A blender is a wonderful tool for the sauce-maker to possess. To be able to produce a good sauce with minimum effort and time helps more than anything to improve the quality of one's cooking. After all, most cooking begins with a simple process like boiling, grilling, baking and so on, but it is the sauce and the flavourings added which make the final dish interesting. The effort of making conventional sauces, especially the more tricky ones like hollandaise or mayonnaise, daunts many cooks, and they fall back on the packet or bottled sauce, or just don't bother. A blender is the solution to this problem.

Even if you make sauces the conventional way the blender is still a boon for removing lumps, blending in skin, rescuing a curdled sauce or smoothing a re-heated frozen sauce. The only precaution necessary is to be careful not to over-blend at this stage or the sauce may become too thin. Just a second or two is usually enough to remedy any defects.

When a completed hot sauce is being blended, warm the goblet first, and then re-heating the sauce should be unnecessary. Do not fill the goblet more than two thirds with sauce and be sure to keep your hand on the lid while switching on the motor.

TWO BASIC METHODS FOR SAUCES WITH A FLOUR OR STARCH THICKENING

1. Melt the fat in a small pan. Use cold liquid and blend flour and seasonings with it. Add to the fat, stir until it boils and simmer for 5 minutes, or longer over boiling water.
2. Use hot liquid and blend all ingredients together. Return to the pan, stir until it boils and cook for 3 minutes, or longer over boiling water.

ANCHOVY SAUCE (for fish)

QUANTITIES for 4 – 8

1 pt hot milk or fish stock or a mixture ($\frac{1}{2}$ l): 2 oz flour (50 g): 2 oz butter or margarine (50 g): 6 – 8 canned anchovy fillets or 2 – 3 tsp anchovy essence

40

Put ingredients in the blender goblet and mix until smooth, a couple of seconds is usually enough. Pour into the pan and stir until it boils. Simmer for 3 minutes.

Lemon juice: Pepper

Before serving add lemon juice to taste and season with pepper. Any left over can be frozen for future use.

AURORA SAUCE

QUANTITIES for 4 – 8

1 pt hot milk ($\frac{1}{2}$ l): 2 oz flour (50 g): 2 oz butter or margarine (50 g)

Blend for a few seconds until smooth, return to the pan and stir until boiling. Simmer for 3 minutes.

2 – 4 Tbs concentrated tomato purée: Salt, pepper and sugar to taste: Cream to taste

Either whisk in by hand just before serving the sauce, or put in the warmed goblet and blend to mix.

Any left over can be frozen for later use.

BÉCHAMEL OR WHITE SAUCE

QUANTITIES for 4 – 8

1 pt milk ($\frac{1}{2}$ l): 1 piece onion: 1 piece carrot: 1 piece celery: 6 – 8 peppercorns: 1 bay leaf

Warm the milk with the flavourings and set aside to infuse for 5 minutes. Strain into the blender goblet.

2 oz flour (50 g): 2 oz butter or margarine (50 g)

Add to the goblet and blend for a few seconds until smooth. Return to the pan and stir until boiling, simmer for 3 minutes.

4 Tbs single cream: Salt

Add just before serving. Any left over can be frozen for future use.

BREAD SAUCE (for poultry)

COOKING TIME: 25 mins. QUANTITIES for 4

2 oz bread without crusts (50 g)

41

Tear the bread in small pieces and blend to make crumbs. Either drop in from the top with the motor running on slow speed or put in with the motor off and blend on/off at slow speed.

1 onion: ½ pt milk (250 ml): 4 cloves

Peel and cut up the onion. Chop it coarsely in the blender with the milk. Put in a small pan with the cloves. Bring to the boil and set aside to infuse for 10 minutes. Strain and add the breadcrumbs, keeping warm for the crumbs to swell.

1 oz butter or margarine (25 g): Salt and pepper

Add the fat and allow to melt. Mix in and season to taste. Serve hot.

CAPER SAUCE (for lamb, mutton and fish)

QUANTITIES for 4 – 8

1 pt hot meat or fish stock or milk (½ l): 2 oz butter or margarine (50 g); 2 oz flour (50 g)

Blend for a few seconds to mix smooth. Return to the pan and stir until it boils. Simmer for 3 minutes.

2 Tbs capers: Vinegar: Salt and pepper

Put the capers in the goblet with enough sauce to cover the blades and blend just to chop the capers. Return to the main sauce, mix, taste for seasoning and add salt, pepper and vinegar to taste. Serve hot.

CELERY SAUCE (for chicken or game)

QUANTITIES for 4 – 6

1 lb can celery hearts (500 g)

Empty into the goblet with the liquid and blend smooth. Strain in case any fibres are left unblended. Put in a pan and heat.

Cream, evaporated milk, white sauce or gravy

Add to the celery to give the desired consistency.

Salt and pepper: Ground mace or nutmeg: Onion salt

Season to taste and serve hot.

CHEESE SAUCE OR SAUCE MORNAY

QUANTITIES for 4 – 8

*2 – 3 oz Parmesan cheese (50 – 75 g) or 4 oz Cheddar or similar
cheese (125 g)*

Cut Parmesan cheese in small pieces and blend it on slow
speed, dropping pieces in from the top. Blend to grate finely. Tip
into a basin. The other cheese is cut in small pieces and blended
with the other ingredients.

*1 pt hot milk (½ l): 2 oz butter or margarine (50 g): 2 oz flour
(50 g): ½ tsp dry mustard: Salt and pepper*

Put in the blender goblet, adding the Cheddar cheese in pieces, if
used. Blend to make smooth and return to the pan. Stir until it
boils and simmer for 3 minutes, adding the Parmesan cheese for
the last minute. Taste for seasoning and serve hot.

CHEESE SAUCE (without flour)

QUANTITIES for 4

*¼ pt evaporated milk (150 ml): 4 oz strong cheese (125 g):
1 tsp French mustard: Salt and pepper: 2 Tbs red wine*

Cut the cheese in pieces and put all in the goblet. Blend until
smooth. Pour into a pan and heat slowly, stirring until amost boiling. Season to taste.

Alternative. For a thicker sauce add an egg yolk when blending
the ingredients.

FISH ROE SAUCE (for herrings or mackerel)

COOKING TIME: a few mins. QUANTITIES for 2 – 4

*Soft or hard roes from 2 herrings or mackerel: 1 tsp dry
mustard: 1 tsp anchovy essence: 1 Tbs vinegar: 2 oz melted
butter or margarine (50 g): 3 Tbs milk: pepper*

Wash the roes and put them in the goblet with the other ingredients. Blend until smooth. Tip into a small pan and heat gently,
stirring frequently, until boiling. Simmer for a few minutes,
adding more milk as required. Serve hot. This is excellent with
fried, boiled or grilled fish.

GREEN DUTCH SAUCE (for fish)

QUANTITIES for 4 – 8

1 pt hot milk or half milk and half fish stock ($\frac{1}{2}$ l): 2 oz butter or margarine (50 g): 2 oz flour (50 g): 2 handsful of parsley sprigs.

Put in the goblet and blend to chop the parsley finely. Return to the pan and stir until it boils. Simmer for 3 minutes.

Salt and pepper: Lemon juice, to taste

Season to taste and serve hot. Any left over sauce can be frozen for future use.

HOLLANDAISE SAUCE

This is the classical Hollandaise adapted to the blender method. It is so quick to make that it can be a last minute job although it will keep warm satisfactorily for some time – but not hot or it will separate.

QUANTITIES for 4

2 egg yolks: 1 Tbs lemon juice: Pinch of salt and pepper

Put in the goblet

4 oz butter (125 g)

Heat the butter in small pan until it just begins to bubble. Blend the egg yolks for a few seconds at high speed. Then remove the top or cap and pour the butter into the eggs in a steady stream with the motor running. Blend for 30 seconds. If desired, dilute with another tablespoon of lemon juice.

WHOLE EGG HOLLANDAISE SAUCE

This makes a thinner sauce than the classical one made with egg yolks. It keeps warm satisfactorily and also makes a good cold sauce for dressing cold chicken or fish, or for a salad.

QUANTITIES for 4

1 egg: 1 Tbs lemon juice: $\frac{1}{4}$ tsp salt: Pinch pepper

Put in the goblet.

2 oz butter (50 g): 1 Tbs boiling water

Heat the butter until it just begins to bubble. Blend the egg for a few seconds. Then remove the top or cap and pour the butter onto the egg in a steady stream with the motor running at full speed. Finally pour in the water and blend for 30 seconds.

MUSHROOM SAUCE

This method gives a pleasant mushroom-pink sauce due to blending the mushrooms finely. It has an excellent flavour.

QUANTITIES for 4

½pt hot milk (250 ml): 3 oz button mushrooms (75 g): ½ oz butter or margarine (1 Tbs): ½ oz flour (1½ Tbs): Salt and pepper

Put all in the blender goblet and mix until the mushrooms are finely chopped. Return to the pan and stir until it boils. Simmer for 3 minutes, season and serve.

ONION SAUCE

COOKING TIME: 30 mins. QUANTITIES for 4

8 oz onions (250 g): 1 oz butter or margarine (25 g)

Skin and slice the onions, or blender-chop them coarsely. Stew them in the melted fat until they are soft not but brown.

1 Tbs flour: ½ pt milk (250 ml): Salt and pepper: Ground nutmeg or mace

Stir the flour into the onions and add the milk. Simmer for 15 minutes or until the onions are cooked. Put in the goblet with the seasoning and blend smooth. This can either be put straight into the sauce boat or kept warm over hot water.

Alternative. Add some cream just before serving the sauce.

PARSLEY SAUCE

QUANTITIES for 4 – 8

4 good sprigs parsley

Wash the parsley and put it in the goblet with 2 tablespoons of cold water. Blend just to chop finely and then pour into a small strainer and set aside.

1 pt hot milk or half milk and half stock (½ l): 2 oz butter or margarine (50 g): 2 oz flour (50 g): Salt and pepper

Put in the goblet and blend for a few seconds. Return to the pan and stir until it boils. Simmer 3 minutes. Taste for seasoning, add the parsley and serve.

PIMENTO SAUCE (for fish, eggs or white meats)

This makes a beautiful orange-coloured sauce with a fine flavour.

QUANTITIES for 4 – 8

1 pt hot milk ($\frac{1}{2}$ l): 2 cooked or canned sweet red peppers or pimentos: 2 oz butter or margarine (50 g): 2 oz flour (50 g)

Put in the goblet and blend smooth. Return to the pan and stir until it boils. Simmer 3 minutes.

Salt and pepper: 4 or more Tbs cream

Season to taste and add the cream just before serving. Any left over can be frozen for future use.

SUPRÊME SAUCE

QUANTITIES for 6 – 8

1 pt milk ($\frac{1}{2}$ l): 1 piece onion: 1 piece carrot: 1 piece celery: 6 – 8 peppercorns: 1 bay leaf

Warm the milk with the flavourings and set aside to infuse for 5 minutes. Strain into the blender goblet.

1 oz flour (25 g): 1 oz butter or margarine (25 g)

Add to the milk and blend until smooth. Return to the pan and stir until it boils. Simmer for 3 minutes.

2 egg yolks: 4 Tbs single cream: Salt and pepper

Put the egg yolks and cream in the goblet and add a little of the hot sauce. Blend a few seconds, add to the rest of the sauce, mix well, season to taste and serve hot.

SWEET PEPPER AND TOMATO SAUCE (for fish or meat)

COOKING TIME: about $\frac{1}{2}$ hr. QUANTITIES for 4

4 oz green or red sweet peppers (125 g): 8 oz tomatoes, fresh or canned (250 g): 2 Tbs water: 2 medium gherkins: 1 Tbs wine vinegar: Salt and pepper

Cut the peppers in pieces, removing the seeds. Cut fresh tomatoes in pieces and cut up the gherkins. Put all in the blender goblet and blend to chop the peppers and gherkins finely. Pour into a pan and simmer gently until the vegetables are tender and the sauce reduced to a pulpy consistency.

TWO QUICK TOMATO SAUCES

No. 1

A 10 oz can condensed tomato soup (250 ml): 1 Tbs tarragon vinegar: 1 tsp brown sugar: 1 tsp Worcester or soya sauce: Salt and pepper

Blend together for a few seconds and then tip into a pan. Bring to the boil, taste for seasoning and serve.

No. 2 (for pasta and general use)

1 lb can peeled tomatoes (500 g): 1 beef or chicken cube: Pinch dried garlic: Pinch rosemary: Pinch thyme: Salt and pepper

Put in the goblet and blend until smooth. Tip into a pan and boil gently until reduced to about half the quantity. Season to taste and serve hot.

VELOUTÉ SAUCE

QUANTITIES for 4 – 8

1 pt hot stock ($\frac{1}{2}$ l), chicken or other white stock or fish stock, according to its use: 2 oz butter or margarine (50 g): 2 oz flour (50 g)

Blend together until smooth. Return to the pan and stir until it boils. Simmer for 3 minutes.

Salt and pepper: Grated nutmeg or mace

Season to taste and serve hot.

COLD SAVOURY SAUCES

BRETON SAUCE (for fish or cold meat)

QUANTITIES for 2 – 4

1 tsp French mustard: 2 egg yolks: 1 Tbs vinegar: $\frac{1}{4}$ tsp salt: Pinch of pepper

Put in the goblet and blend for a few seconds.

2 oz almost melted butter (50 g)

Add and mix for 30 seconds.

Fresh green herbs to taste

Break up in pieces and add, blending just long enough to chop them. Tip into a small sauce boat and leave to become cold when it will thicken considerably.

CREAM CHEESE DRESSING

This can be used in place of mayonnaise. The paprika pepper makes it pink but there is no reason why it should not be left out and other pepper substituted. It could also be made into a green dressing by blending in a sprig of parsley instead of the paprika pepper. When just made the sauce is of a pouring consistency but thickens on cooling and after refrigeration it may need to have some more oil or lemon beaten in to thin it.

¼ pt oil (150 ml): 3 Tbs lemon juice: 4 oz cream cheese (125 g): Pinch of garlic salt: ½ tsp salt: ½ tsp paprika pepper

Put all in the goblet and blend until smooth and creamy.

CURRY SAUCE

This is a thin sauce, delicious with cold poultry. Serve it separately, or remove the meat from the bone, arrange it in a serving dish and pour the sauce over it.

QUANTITIES for 6 – 8

3 – 4 oz apple (75 – 100 g): 4 Tbs olive oil: ¼ of a green pepper: 2 Tbs lemon juice: ½ tsp celery salt: ¼ tsp sugar: Pinch of thyme: Pinch of cayenne pepper: ¼ pt white wine (150 ml): 1 Tbs curry powder: Pinch dried garlic

Peel and core the apple and cut it up roughly. Remove seeds and cut the pepper in strips. Put all the ingredients in the goblet and mix until smooth.

ENGLISH SALAD DRESSING

This looks like mayonnaise and is a good alternative for those who dislike oil.

QUANTITIES for 4

¼ pt cream, top milk or evaporated milk (150 ml): 2 hardboiled egg yolks: ¼ tsp salt: ¼ tsp caster sugar: Pinch of cayenne pepper: 1–2 Tbs vinegar or lemon juice

Put all the ingredients in the goblet and blend for 30 seconds. Adjust the vinegar or lemon juice to taste and to vary the thickness.

Alternative. In place of the cream use 6 Tbs olive oil.

HERB SALAD DRESSING

This is a good way of adding the flavour of herbs to a salad as they mix in better than when chopped separately and sprinkled over. It is very good with potato salad.

QUANTITIES for a salad for 8

6 Tbs olive oil: 2 Tbs vinegar: 3 Tbs lemon juice: 1 tsp sugar: ½ tsp salt: Pinch of pepper: ½ small onion, cut up: Fresh herbs to taste

For the herbs you might use a good sprig of parsley, a few tarragon leaves, a few rosemary leaves, a sprig of thyme, and a sprig of marjoram.

Put all the ingredients in the goblet and blend to chop the herbs. Blending emulsifies the oil and produces a creamy dressing. This will stand for a while before separating into oil and vinegar layers.

When this happens, stir before using.

MAYONNAISE

The traditional mayonnaise has always been made with egg yolks only and it can be made in the blender this way, using 2 egg yolks instead of the whole egg in the recipe. I find the whole egg gives better results in the blender and has the advantage of solving the problem of what to do with the egg whites. Mayonnaise made with a whole egg is usually a little paler in colour than one made with yolks. The secret of success, whether yolks or whole egg are used, is to have all ingredients at room temperature; and to stop the blender as soon as the mixture thickens.

1 egg (at room temperature): 2 Tbs lemon juice: 1 tsp French mustard: Pinch sugar: Pinch salt

Put all in the blender goblet. If the egg has come straight out of the refrigerator or cold larder, put it in a bowl of warm water for a few minutes.

¼ – ½ pt oil (150 – 250 ml)

Set the motor running on top speed. Then either remove the lid or the cap provided and let the oil run through in a steady stream until the mayonnaise becomes thick. Stop at once. The mixture will become even thicker when it cools. Turn into a container with a lid and store in the refrigerator. Additional lemon juice or vinegar can be added to taste.

CURRY MAYONNAISE (for vegetables, meat or fish salad)

To $\frac{1}{2}$ pt mayonnaise (250 ml) add 1 – 2 Tbs curry powder and mix well.

MINT SAUCE

QUANTITIES for 4 or more

$\frac{1}{2}$ pt washed mint leaves (250 ml): 2 oz caster sugar (50 g): 4 Tbs malt or wine vinegar

Put in the blender goblet and process at low speed, turning on/off until the mint is finely chopped. Use at once or leave to stand.

RICH MUSTARD SAUCE

(to serve with fish, especially smoked haddock; or with cold meats)

QUANTITIES for 4 – 6

2 oz butter or margarine (50 g): 1 Tbs dry mustard: 2 eggs: 1 tsp salt: Pinch pepper: 2 Tbs vinegar: $\frac{1}{4}$ pt evaporated milk (150 ml)

Melt the fat but don't make it hot. Put all ingredients in the goblet and blend until mixed. Tip into a small pan and cook over boiling water or a very gentle heat, stirring constantly until thick. Serve warm or cold. It should be the consistency of mayonnaise. If it should go lumpy give it a brisk whisk to restore the texture, or blend for a second.

SHARP MUSTARD SAUCE
(for ham, corned beef, boiled meats and fish)

QUANTITIES for 4

1 Tbs flour: 2 Tbs dry mustard: 1 Tbs sugar: $\frac{1}{2}$ tsp salt: 1 egg: $\frac{1}{4}$ pt milk (150 ml)

Put all in the goblet and blend until smooth. Put in a pan and heat gently, stirring frequently, until it thickens.

$\frac{1}{4}$ pt cider or wine vinegar and water mixed (150 ml)

Use three parts vinegar to one part of water, or to taste. Add to the other ingredients, stir until it boils, and simmer for several minutes, stirring all the time. Serve warm or cold.

SALSA VERDE

This is the Italian green sauce, traditionally served with Il Bollito Misto, but also suitable for serving with other boiled meats, cold meat, or poached fish.

QUANTITIES for 4 – 6

4 Tbs olive oil: ¼ pt wine vinegar (150 ml): 2 oz parsley (50 g): 1 oz drained rinsed capers (25 g): 1 oz pickled gherkins (25 g): 1 oz bread (25 g) or 1 small potato: Salt, pepper, pinch sugar

Cut the parsley, including the stalks, roughly. Cut up the gherkins, remove the crusts from the bread and break it in pieces, cut up the potato if used. Blend to chop the parsley. Serve cold.

SOUR CREAM DRESSING

QUANTITIES for 4

2 hard boiled eggs: 1 tsp salt: ¼ pt soured or cultured cream (150 ml): ¼ tsp pepper: 1 tsp dry mustard

Separate the whites and yolks of the eggs, reserving the whites for garnishing the salad. Put all the ingredients in the blender goblet and mix until smooth.

TARTARE SAUCE

½ pt mayonnaise (250 ml): 1 slice of onion: 2 small gherkins or 2 Tbs capers

Cut the gherkins in 2 or 3 pieces. If capers are used, rinse them. Put all in the blender goblet and blend to chop the onion and gherkin finely.

VIENNESE EGG SAUCE OR SAUCE GRIBISCHE

This is very good served with cold or hot fish, hot roast or boiled meats and cold meat.

QUANTITIES for 6 – 8

3 hard boiled egg yolks: 3 Tbs olive oil: ¼ tsp salt: 3 Tbs tarragon vinegar: ½ tsp sugar: 1 sprig parsley: Few chives: 1 Tbs French mustard

Put all in the goblet and blend until smooth.

3 hard boiled egg whites

Cut the whites in quarters and add to the sauce, blend on/off to chop them. Pour into a sauce boat and leave to stand for a while before serving.

VINAIGRETTE SAUCE

(for asparagus, artichokes, calf's head and other meats)

These are the ingredients of classical Vinaigrette sauce but the blender makes the oil emulsify and the sauce is of a creamy texture. It stays like this for several hours, it tastes as usual and is easier to serve.

QUANTITIES for 8

¼ *pt olive oil (150 ml): 4 Tbs tarragon vinegar: 1 small gherkin, sliced: 1 slice of onion: 2 sprigs of parsley: ¼ tsp salt: Pinch of pepper: 1 tsp French mustard*

Blend just enough to chop the onion and gherkin finely.

SWEET SAUCES

APRICOT GLAZE

This is used for glazing fruit in a flan or as a sauce for fresh raw fruit, for glazing baked apples, for brushing the sides of a fruit cake before putting on the almond paste, or for brushing cakes before sprinkling with chopped nuts.

3 oz apricot jam (75 g): 2 Tbs hot water

Put in the goblet and blend until smooth. Brush over fruit or cake.

Alternative. As a glaze for fruit, other jams of appropriate flavours can be used in the same way. Marmalade glaze is useful in many cases.

BANANA SAUCE (for ices, puddings and fruit)

QUANTITIES for 4 – 6

4 small ripe bananas: ½ pt single cream (250 ml): 2 Tbs lemon juice: Caster sugar to taste

Peel the bananas and cut them in several pieces. Put in the goblet with the other ingredients and mix smooth, about 30 seconds. Serve at once as the colour takes on a brownish tinge if the sauce is kept for any time.

CHERRY SAUCE

(for ices, baked or steamed puddings or fruit salad)

QUANTITIES for 4

8 oz can of cherries or 8 oz cherries, stewed (250 g): 4 oz red current jelly: Kirsch to taste

Strain the fruit and remove the stones. Heat the juice to boiling. Put the jelly in the blender goblet and pour in the hot juice. Blend just enough to melt the jelly, too long will make it very frothy.

Add the cherries and blend to make smooth. Flavour to taste and serve hot or cold.

CHOCOLATE SAUCE (for hot or cold puddings)

QUANTITIES for 6 – 8

2 Tbs cornflour: 3 Tbs sugar: Pinch salt: 2 Tbs cocoa powder: 1 Tbs soluble coffee: 1 pt milk (500 ml)

Put the ingredients in the goblet and blend for a few seconds to mix smoothly. Pour into a pan and stir until the mixture thickens and boils. Simmer for 3 minutes.

Vanilla essence: Single or double cream

Flavour to taste and add the cream just before serving.

QUICK CHOCOLATE SAUCE

This makes a fairly thin hot sauce ideal for ices, or cold or hot puddings. When refrigerated it thickens and can be used as it is or diluted with milk or cream.

QUANTITIES for 4 or more

4 oz semi-sweet or bitter chocolate (125 g): ¼ pt hot milk (150 ml): Pinch of salt: Vanilla, rum or brandy to taste

Break the chocolate in small pieces and put it in the goblet with the other ingredients. Blend smooth, about 20 seconds. Use at once for a hot sauce or allow it to become cold, and then store in the refrigerator.

MOCHA SAUCE

Add 1 tsp of soluble coffee before blending, or use more coffee if you like a strong flavour.

CHOCOLATE PEPPERMINT SAUCE

Add peppermint essence to taste.

CUSTARD SAUCE

This is a better sauce than one made with custard powder but it is not as tricky as a real egg custard sauce.

COOKING TIME: 2 – 3 mins. QUANTITIES for 4 – 8

1 pt hot milk ($\frac{1}{2}$ l): 1 egg: 1 oz butter (25 g): 2 oz sugar (50 g): 2 Tbs cornflour: $\frac{1}{2}$ tsp vanilla essence

Put half the hot milk in the goblet with the other ingredients. Blend for 30 seconds or until thoroughly mixed. Return to the pan with the rest of the milk. Stir until the sauce thickens and boils. Simmer for 2 – 3 minutes. Use hot or cold. To get rid of the skin which forms as the sauce becomes cold, blend a second before serving, and, if required, dilute with milk or cream.

Alternative. Use potato flour in place of the cornflour, in which case the sauce will be cooked as soon as it boils.

RAW FRUIT SAUCE

QUANTITIES for 4

8 oz raw ripe fruit (250 g): Caster or icing sugar to taste

Juicy fruits such as cherries, black and red currants, raspberries, strawberries, and other berries, are the best to use. Partially thawed frozen fruit is also suitable. Wash fresh fruit and remove stones and stalks. Blend to make a smooth pulp, adding sugar to taste. Strain to remove pips if necessary. If it becomes frothy during blending, leave to stand for a while before serving.

The sauces can be served either hot or cold, and diluted to taste with sugar syrup, see page 151.

The addition of a little Kirsch or other liqueur is often an improvement.

COOKED FRUIT SAUCE

Use canned or stewed fruit. Best ones are apricot, blackcurrant, greengage, raspberry, loganberry or strawberry. Drain the fruit and remove any stones. Put fruit and its syrup in the blender goblet and blend to a smooth pulp.

Put in a pan and boil rapidly until the sauce thickens enough just to coat the back of a wooden spoon. Flavour to taste with essence or liqueur.

When the sauce is served hot, add a knob of butter.

JAM SAUCE

The blender turns any kind of jam into a smooth sauce for cold or hot puddings.

QUANTITIES for 4 or more

4 oz jam (125 g): 2 tsp lemon juice: ½ pt cold or hot water (250 ml): ½ Tbs potato starch: Liqueur to taste, optional

Put ingredients in the goblet and blend for a few seconds to mix and purée the jam. Tip into a small pan and stir until it boils. Remove immediately from the heat and serve warm or cold.

MARMALADE SAUCE

Make in the same way as Jam Sauce but use chunky marmalade or blender marmalade, and omit the lemon juice.

Alternative, to either Jam or Marmalade Sauce, but using more jam. Put the preserve in the goblet and add an equal volume of boiling water. Blend to mix and serve hot or cold.

JELLY SAUCE (for ices or other puddings)

QUANTITIES for 4

4 oz red currant jelly (125 g): 2 Tbs boiling water: 3 Tbs port or sherry: 2 tsp lemon juice

Put all in the goblet and blend until the jelly is dissolved. It develops a frothy top but this soon subsides. Serve hot or cold.

Alternative. If a thickened sauce is preferred, blend 1 tsp potato starch with it. Bring to the boil and serve hot or cold.

LEMON OR ORANGE SAUCE

COOKING TIME: 5 mins. QUANTITIES for 4

1 small orange or lemon

Pare off the outside rind as thinly as possible. Put the strips in the goblet. Peel off the white pith and discard it. Cut or slice the fruit, removing the pips. Put flesh and juice in the goblet.

½ pt water (250 ml): 2 oz sugar (50 g) or to taste: 2–3 Tbs cornflour

Add to the goblet and process at full speed until the peel is finely chopped, about 1 minute. Pour into a pan and stir until it boils. Boil for 3 minutes. Serve hot or cold, thinning the sauce if necessary with water or fruit juice.

CREAMY ORANGE SAUCE
(for ices and steamed or baked puddings)

QUANTITIES for 4

¼ pt evaporated milk (150 ml): 2 Tbs lemon juice: 1 oz sugar (25 g): Peel of ½ orange: Flesh and juice of 1 orange

Remove the outside peel of half the orange as thinly as possible. Put the strips in the goblet. Remove and discard the white pith and pips of the fruit and put flesh and juice in the goblet with the other ingredients. Blend at high speed for 1 minute.

Serve cold, or heat gently, without boiling, and serve hot or warm.

MELBA SAUCE

This is the sauce for Peach Melba but is also useful for other ices and as a sauce for fresh or frozen strawberries and raspberries.

COOKING TIME: 10 – 15 mins. QUANTITIES for 4 or more

¾ lb fresh or frozen raspberries (375 g)

Partially thaw frozen berries and put fresh or frozen in the goblet and reduce to a pulp. Strain to remove any unblended pips.

½ Tbs cornflour or potato flour

Blend with a little cold water and add to the fruit. Heat and stir until it boils. Cook cornflour for a few minutes. The potato flour is cooked as soon as it boils.

Sugar: Lemon juice

Add to taste. Cool and store in a covered jar in the refrigerator. Use cold.

STUFFINGS

Using a blender for making fine breadcrumbs and blending in the herbs and other flavourings gives a quality of stuffing only obtained in the past by long and laborious processes.

To those who have not had time to do this sort of cooking, and who only know packet stuffings, the possibility of blender mixtures will come as a pleasant surprise.

The breadcrumbs can be from fresh or stale bread, the only difference being that the latter will need more liquid to bind the mixture and moisten the crumbs.

Blend the bread in several lots with the flavourings such as herbs, lemon rind, onion, bacon and so on. This ensures that the flavourings are well distributed.

Alternatively, the flavourings can be blended with the egg or other liquid used for binding the crumbs together.

BACON AND NUT STUFFING FOR FISH

This can be used to stuff a whole large fish or small ones. It is very good used as a stuffing for rolled fillets. Pack the rolls in a flat baking dish, pour a little white wine in to moisten and bake.

QUANTITIES for 4

1 oz bread (25 g): 1 oz hazel nuts (25 g)

Tear the bread in pieces and blend to make fine crumbs. Tip into a bowl. Blend the nuts to chop them finely and add them to the crumbs.

1 rasher bacon: 1 slice onion

Cut the bacon in pieces and fry it until the fat begins to run. Add the onion and fry until it begins to brown. Put both in the blender goblet.

1 sprig parsley: ½ Tbs lemon juice: ¼ tsp celery salt: Pinch of pepper: A few tarragon leaves or fresh savory: 1 egg

Put all in the goblet and blend to chop the herbs. Add to the crumbs and nuts and mix thoroughly.

CHEESE AND ROSEMARY STUFFING (for roast lamb)

QUANTITIES for a 3 – 4 lb shoulder (1½ – 2 kg)

2 oz bread (50 g): 1 oz hard cheese (25 g)

Break up the bread, including the crusts, and make into fine crumbs by dropping pieces through the top with the motor running on slow speed. Tip into a bowl. Cut the cheese in small pieces and blend at slow speed to grate it. Add to the crumbs. If the blender is a large one the bread and cheese can be processed together.

2 oz onion (50 g): 1 tsp tomato paste: 2 Tbs fresh rosemary leaves or ½ Tbs dried: ½ oz melted butter (1 Tbs): 2 Tbs white wine: 1 egg: ½ tsp salt: Pinch pepper

Skin the onion and cut it in two or three pieces. Put all the ingredients in the goblet and blend to chop the fresh herbs and onions. Add to the breadcrumbs and cheese and mix well, adding more wine if needed to bind the ingredients together.

MUSHROOM STUFFING (for poultry)

QUANTITIES for a 3½ – 4 lb chicken (1½ – 2 kg)

2 oz butter (50 g): 4 oz sliced mushrooms (125 g)

Heat the butter and fry the mushrooms gently for a few minutes. Leave to cool a little.

4 oz crustless bread (125 g): Yellow rind of 1 lemon

Break the bread in pieces and blend it to crumbs in one or more lots, blending strips of lemon peel with each lot, until all the peel is finely chopped. Tip into a bowl.

½ – 1 tsp salt: Pinch of cayene pepper: 1 egg

Put in the blender goblet with the mushrooms and their liquid. Blend just to chop the mushrooms. Add to the dry mixture.

Wine or lemon juice

Rinse out the goblet with a tablespoon of wine or lemon juice and add to the stuffing, with more liquid if needed, the amount needed depending on the dryness of the breadcrumbs used.

SAGE AND ONION STUFFING (for duck, pork or goose)

This is a variation on the standard sage and onion stuffing. It makes a very soft, well-flavoured stuffing. It you prefer a more solid mixture, simply increase the quantity of breadcrumbs. Make well in advance to allow time for it to cool before stuffing the bird or meat.

QUANTITIES for 1 duck (double the recipe for a goose)

1lb onions (500 g): 18 fresh sage leaves

Peel the onions and cut them in pieces if they are large ones. Wash the sage leaves and put onions and sage in the blender goblet with cold water to cover. Process to chop the onion fairly finely. Drain well.

1 oz butter or margarine (25 g)

Melt the fat in a small pan and stew the onion mixture in it until soft and transparent. Stir frequently.

2 oz bread (50 g): 1 tsp salt: ¼ tsp pepper

Break the bread in small pieces, including the crusts. Drop through the top of the blender with the motor running at slow speed and blend until fine. Add to the onions and add the seasoning. Stir and cook for 3 – 4 minutes longer for the crumbs to absorb moisture. Cool before using.

WALNUT STUFFING (for veal or poultry)

QUANTITIES for a small turkey or large chicken.

4 oz bread without crusts (125 g): 4 oz shelled walnuts (125 g)

Break the bread in pieces and feed it through the top of the goblet with the motor running at slow speed. When the motor begins to slow up, stop and tip the crumbs into a bowl. Repeat until all the crumbs are done. Blend the walnuts in one or two lots using the on/off technique, just to chop them. Add to the breacrumbs.

2 oz packet suet (50 g)

Add to the crumbs and nuts and mix.

1 onion, quartered: 1 sprig of parsley: 1 sprig of thyme: 1 strip of yellow lemon rind: 1 tsp salt: Pinch of pepper: 1 large egg: Raw liver of the poultry, cut up

Put in the goblet and blend to chop the herbs, liver and lemon. Pour into the bowl and mix the stuffing thoroughly, adding milk if more moisture is needed.

Chapter Seven

BATTERS

Batters for pancakes, Yorkshire pudding, fritters and drop scones can all be blended quickly, easily and with excellent results.

The ingredients are all put in the goblet together and processed for a minute on fast speed. Some people advise putting the eggs in the goblet first, then the flour and lastly the liquid, the idea being that flour is less likely to stick to the sides of the goblet this way. I find it makes little difference which way one adds the ingredients, and it is always easy to stop the motor and scrape the sides if needed.

BASIC PANCAKE RECIPE

QUANTITIES for 6 – 8 pancakes

2 eggs: 4 oz plain flour (125 g): ½ tsp salt: ½ pt milk (250 ml)

Put the ingredients in the goblet and blend on high speed for one minute, scraping down if necessary.

Turn into a jug or bowl. It is ready to use right away without any standing.

Heat a small knob of lard in a 7 inch (18 cm) pan and, when it is hot, pour out any surplus. Pour in enough batter to make a thin film on the pan and adjust the heat to moderate. When the pancake is brown on one side turn or toss and brown the other side.

STUFFED PANCAKES (using cooked meat)

QUANTITIES for 8 pancakes

8 oz cooked meat (250 g): Salt and pepper: ½ pt sauce or gravy (250 ml): Garlic or onion salt

Remove skin and gristle from the meat and cut the meat in small pieces. Blend it in one or more lots to shred it finely and heat it with the sauce or gravy and seasoning. As the pancakes are made, put a little filling on each. Roll up and put to keep hot.

If liked, put them in a baking dish and sprinkle the tops with cheese grated in the blender. Heat under the grill to melt the cheese, and brown the top.

LAYERED MEAT PANCAKES

QUANTITIES for 4

8 oz cold cooked meat (250 g)

Remove all fat and gristle from the meat, cut the meat in pieces and blend in one or more lots to shred it finely.

½ pt brown sauce, mushroom sauce, or an appropriate condensed soup (250 ml): Pinch of grated nutmeg: 1 Tbs lemon juice: Salt and pepper: Garlic salt, optional

Heat meat, sauce and flavourings to boiling and simmer for a few minutes. Keep hot while making the pancakes. Use the basic pancake recipe and make them not less than 8 in. in size (20 cm). As they are cooked, put the first one on a hot plate, spread with a layer of the meat mixture and repeat the layers, placing the top pancake with its good side uppermost. To serve, cut in wedges like a cake. Green salad makes a good accompaniment.

PANCAKES STUFFED WITH PORK

QUANTITIES for 4

8 oz cold cooked pork (250 g)

Trim off skin, gristle and surplus fat and cut the pork in small pieces. Blend to mince the meat and tip it into a bowl. With most blenders this will need to be done in two or more lots.

½ pt apple sauce or gravy or other sauce (250 ml): 1 slice of onion: 2 sage leaves or a pinch of dried: 1 tsp salt: Pepper: Pinch of ground nutmeg: 1 – 2 Tbs wine

Put all in the goblet and blend to chop the onion and sage. Combine with the meat, adding more sauce or wine as needed to moisten the meat. Heat to boiling and simmer for a few minutes. Keep hot while making the pancakes. Put a little of the filling on each one and roll up. When all are finished put in a dish in a moderate oven to make sure they are hot before serving.

SMOKED HADDOCK AND PIMENTO PANCAKES

QUANTITIES for 4

8 oz smoked haddock (250 g)

Cook the fish, remove skin and bones, flake and set aside

1 pt hot milk (½ l): 2 cooked or canned sweet red peppers or pimentos: 2 oz butter or margarine (50 g): 2 oz flour (50 g)

Put in the goblet and blend smooth. Return to the pan and stir until it boils. Simmer 3 minutes.

Salt and pepper: 4 or more Tbs cream

Season to taste and add the cream. Mix half the sauce with the fish, heat to boiling and keep hot. Keep the remaining sauce hot.

Basic pancake recipe page 60.

Make the pancakes and pile them on each other, keeping them warm. When all are made, spread a little of the fish mixture on each, roll up and pack close together in a shallow baking dish. Pour the remaining sauce over the top and put the dish in the oven at a moderate heat for 15 – 20 minutes to make sure the pancakes are hot. Serve garnished with

Strips of cooked or canned red pepper.

BASIC SWEET PANCAKES

QUANTITIES for 8 pancakes

2 eggs: 4 oz plain flour (125 g): 1 oz caster sugar (25 g): ½ pt milk (250 ml)

Put all in the goblet and blend for 1 minute, scraping down if necessary. Heat a little lard in an 8 in. (20 cm) pan and when hot pour out surplus. Put in enough batter to make a thin coating on the bottom of the pan. Cook until brown, turn or toss, and brown the other side. Serve plain with lemon juice and caster sugar or spread with a fruit purée or jam and roll up.

BANANA PANCAKES

QUANTITIES for 8 pancakes

2 large bananas: 1 Tbs lemon juice: Caster sugar to taste

Peel the bananas and cut in pieces. Blend to a smooth purée with the lemon and sugar. Put in a small bowl. Use the sweet pancake recipe and, as each one is cooked, spread it with some of the banana mixture, roll up and keep hot. Serve sprinkled with caster sugar.

DUTCH LAYERED PANCAKES

This is not a last minute job like most pancakes but is made in advance and served cold: unusual and very good.

QUANTITIES for 4

1 lb well flavoured apples (500 g): Ground cinnamon: Sugar

Peel and core the apples and stew them with the minimum amount of water until they are just tender. Blend them to a purée with sugar and cinnamon to taste. If the purée is wet and sloppy, heat the mixture to drive off excess moisture. Leave to cool.

2 eggs: 4 oz flour (125 g): 1 oz caster sugar (25 g): ½ pt milk (250 ml)

Put in the goblet and process at high speed for 1 minute. Use the batter to make 8 pancakes about 7 inches (18 cm) in diameter. As each is made put it on the serving dish, sandwiching them in a pile with the apple mixture between each layer. Allow to become almost cold.

Icing sugar: Cream or custard sauce

Sprinkle the top thickly with icing sugar and cut in wedges like a cake when serving. Hand the cream or custard sauce separately.

DROP SCONES OR SCOTCH PANCAKES

COOKING TIME: 3 – 4 mins. each batch. QUANTITIES for 24 scones

2 eggs: 1 oz sugar (25 g): 4 oz self-raising flour (125 g): ¼ tsp salt: ½ oz melted butter or margarine (1 Tbs): ¼ pt milk (150 ml)

Put all in the blender goblet and process for 30 seconds. Heat a girdle or heavy frying pan and grease it slightly with lard or oil. Drop the batter from the tip of a tablespoon to make small rounds. Cook until bubbles appear on the top, turn, and cook the other side until brown. If the heat is right they should be cooked through by the time they are browned. Serve with butter, jam, honey or syrup.

FRITTER BATTER

COOKING TIME: 10 – 15 mins. QUANTITIES for 8 fritters

1 egg: 4 oz self-raising flour (125 g): 1 tsp salt: ¼ pt milk (150 ml)

Put the egg in the goblet, then the flour, salt, and milk. Blend on high speed for 1 minute. Use for coating apples, bananas and other fruit fritters. Fry in shallow or deep fat.

CHEESE FRITTERS

2 – 3 oz well-flavoured cheese (50 – 75 g)

Cut the cheese in pieces and blend it with the other ingredients. Fry spoonfuls in hot fat or oil and serve as an accompaniment to meat, or by themselves with a sauce, such as tomato.

CORN FRITTERS

3 oz drained canned or cooked corn (75 g)

Mix the corn with the finished batter and drop spoonfuls in hot fat. Fry until brown. Usually served with chicken dishes. If preferred, the corn can be blended with the other ingredients to give the corn flavour without whole pieces of corn.

FISH OR MEAT FRITTERS

3 oz cooked meat or fish (75 g)

The meat may be cut in small dice and the fish flaked, and then mixed with the finished batter. Alternatively, blend the meat to mince it finely and then add to the batter. Fry in spoonfuls in hot fat until brown. Serve with an appropriate sauce such as tomato, cheese or brown sauce.

Chapter Eight

EGGS

The main use of the blender in egg cookery is to speed up the mixing of eggs and other ingredients as in batters, soufflés, cold sweets, hot puddings, sauces, mayonnaise and in many other types of recipe.

It can be used to whisk eggs for omelets and scrambled eggs, giving a light, frothy mixture only obtained with long beating. Flavouring can be blended in at the same time though I find one needs to be careful or the added ingredients spoil the typical egg flavour of these dishes. I find it excellent for the basic mixture and also for adding cheese and herbs but prefer other flavourings to be added in larger pieces during cooking.

Egg yolks can be whisked with a little cold water (1 Tbs per yolk). Egg whites can be broken up for mixing purposes but will not beat properly for meringues or folding into soufflés or other similar recipes. For this they must be beaten separately, by hand, or with an electric beater.

BUCK RAREBIT

QUANTITIES for 4

8 oz Cheddar or Cheshire cheese (250 g)

Cut the cheese in 1 inch (2 cm) cubes and blend in two or more lots to grate it finely. Tip into a small saucepan.

1 oz soft or melted butter (25 g): 4 Tbs milk or ale: 1 tsp made mustard: Pinch cayenne pepper or 1 tsp Worcester sauce

Add to the cheese and stir over a gentle heat until the mixture is smooth.

4 slices toast: 4 poached eggs

Butter the toast or leave it plain. Cover with the cheese mixture and serve with the poached egg on top.

COTTAGE CHEESE OMELET

COOKING TIME: a few mins. QUANTITIES for 4

4 egg yolks: 4 oz cottage cheese (125 g): ½ tsp salt: 1 sprig parsley: Pinch of pepper

Put in the blender goblet and mix until smooth and creamy. If it seems too thick, add a little milk or cream.

4 egg whites

Beat until stiff, add the blended mixture and fold together.

1 oz butter (25 g)

Heat in a large, 10 inch (25 cm), frying pan and add the omelet mixture. Cook slowly until brown underneath and beginning to rise in the pan. Then grill the top gently to dry it. Fold over and put on a large hot serving dish, to be divided at table; or cut into portions and serve on individual hot plates.

EGG AND ANCHOVY SALAD

QUANTITIES for 4

1 lettuce: 4 tomatoes

Wash and put to drain.

1 hard boiled egg: 1 slice of onion: 8 anchovy fillets or a 2 oz can (50 g): 2 Tbs oil: 2 Tbs lemon juice: Pinch of pepper: ¼ tsp dry mustard

Shell and quarter the egg. Cut anchovy fillets in half. Put all in the goblet and blend to chop the egg and anchovy. Tear or shred the lettuce and cut up the tomatoes. Arrange in a salad bowl and pour the dressing over the lettuce.

Alternatives.
1. Use cooked cauliflower sprigs in place of the lettuce and to-mato.
2. Use the egg and anchovy mixture as a dressing in place of mayonnaise for an egg salad.

66

EGGS CRÉCY

COOKING TIME: 20 – 30 mins. QUANTITIES for 4

1 lb carrots (500 g): 1 oz butter or margarine (25 g): Salt and pepper

Boil the carrots until tender and then blend them to a pulp with the fat and seasoning. Alternatively, use an equal weight of canned carrots, blend and heat with fat and seasoning. Put the carrots in the bottom of a shallow baking dish, large enough to take 4 poached eggs; or arrange the carrots in mounds on four separate dishes. Keep hot.

1 pt milk (500 ml), or use some milk and some carrot stock: A piece each of onion and celery: 1 bay leaf

Heat together and allow to stand for 5 minutes to infuse. Strain into the goblet.

1½ oz flour (40 g): 1½ oz butter or margarine (40 g): Salt and pepper: 4 Tbs cream

Add to the milk and blend until smooth. Pour into a pan and stir until it boils. Simmer for 3 – 4 minutes. Season to taste and keep warm.

4 eggs: Chopped parsley

Poach the eggs and put them on top of the hot carrot purée. Cover with the sauce and sprinkle with chopped parsley.

OMELET

QUANTITIES for I

2 standard or 1 large egg: 1 Tbs water: Salt and Pepper

Put in the goblet and blend for about 15 seconds.

½ oz butter (1 Tbs)

Heat in the omelet pan until it begins to brown. Add the egg mixture and continue to cook quickly, lifting the edges with a knife to allow the mixture to run underneath. When set, but still creamy, fold over away from the handle and tip onto a hot plate.

OMELET FOR TWO

Use 3 eggs and make the omelet in a 7 – 8 inch (18 – 20 cm) pan. Cut in half for serving.

CHEESE OMELET

Add an inch (2 cm) cube of well-flavoured cheese to the eggs, with a pinch of mustard and blend all together until the cheese is finely grated.

HERB OMELET

Add 1 sprig of parsley, tiny sprig of thyme and 2 or 3 marjoram leaves and blend with the eggs, just to chop the herbs, or use other herbs to taste.

SCRAMBLED EGGS

COOKING TIME: 5 mins. QUANTITIES for 4

4 eggs: ½ tsp salt: Pinch of pepper: 4 Tbs milk

Put in the goblet and blend for a few seconds until the mixture is light and frothy.

1 oz butter or margarine (25 g): 4 slices toast

Melt the fat in a small pan and add the egg mixture. Cook over a low heat stirring once or twice to make a soft creamy mixture. Serve on the hot toast.

SCRAMBLED EGGS WITH CHEESE

1 oz cheese (25 g), cut in pieces

Blend with the eggs in the above recipe, mixing until smooth. Cook as before.

SCRAMBLED EGGS WITH HERBS

Add to the blended eggs a few herbs such as parsley, chervil, chives or tarragon, or a mixture. Blend just to chop the herbs. Cook as before. If you add the herbs before first blending the eggs they will be chopped too finely and make the egg an unappetising colour.

SWISS EGGS

A quickly made and very delicious egg dish for a light meal. Serve it with salad.

COOKING TIME: 5 – 10 mins. QUANTITIES for 2 – 4

4 eggs; 2 thin slices of onion: 1 sprig of parsley: ½ tsp salt: Pinch of pepper: 1½ oz soft or melted butter or margarine (40 g): 1½ oz cheese, cut in pieces (40 g)

Put all in the goblet and blend for 1 minute. Heat a knob of butter in a 7–8 in. (18 – 20 cm) frying pan. Pour in the egg mixture and cook it fairly slowly, without stirring, until it is brown underneath and almost set through.

Finish the top by browning under the grill. If your grill is not suitable for this, continue cooking until it is set right to the top. Cut in wedges to serve.

Chapter Nine

SAVOURY MOUSSES AND SOUFFLÉS

A good mousse should have a fine smooth texture, more quickly achieved by using a blender than by any other method. Cream, evaporated milk or mayonnaise can be blended with the basic ingredients but egg whites should be beaten separately before being added in the usual way.

Using a blender for soufflés means that the egg yolk mixture can be prepared more quickly than by the conventional method. The flavouring ingredients are also easier to prepare, either by shredding dry and adding to the egg yolk mixture, or by blending with it, as with cheese soufflé. The egg whites must, however, be beaten separately and added in the usual way.

BLUE CHEESE MOUSSE

Suitable for a buffet party or for the main course in a light meal, with salad; or use in place of cheese at the end of a meal.

QUANTITIES for 6 or more

½ oz butter or margarine (1 Tbs): ½ oz flour (1½ Tbs): ¼ pt hot milk (150 ml)

Put in the goblet and blend to mix. Pour into the saucepan and stir until it boils. Simmer for a couple of minutes.

2 Tbs hot water: ½ oz gelatine (1½ Tbs)

Put the water in the goblet and sprinkle in the gelatine. Add the hot sauce and blend for a second to two.

Salt and pepper: Celery salt: 4 oz broken up blue cheese (125 g)

Add to the goblet and blend to make smooth. Pour into a bowl and leave to become quite cold.

¼ pt double cream (150 ml)

Whip the cream lightly and fold it into the cold cheese mixture. Pour into a mould and leave to set, covered in the refrigerator. Unmould and garnish with salad.

Alternative. Line the mould with ¼ pt (150 ml) aspic jelly and set this before adding the mousse mixture.

CHICKEN MOUSSE

QUANTITIES for 6

8 oz cold cooked chicken (250 g) or use some chicken and some ham

Remove all skin, gristle and bone and cut the chicken in small pieces.

½ oz gelatine (1½ Tbs): ¼ pt hot chicken stock (150 ml)

Put the stock in the goblet and add the gelatine. Blend for a few seconds.

¼ pt evaporated milk (150 ml)

Add to the goblet with half the chicken and blend until smooth.

¼ pt mayonnaise (150 ml): ½ tsp salt: Pinch of cayenne pepper: 1 tsp horseradish sauce

Add to the goblet with the rest of the chicken and blend smooth. If this seems too much for the blender, tip out some of the mixture and do it separately. Pour into an oiled mould and, when cold, cover and store in the refrigerator. Unmould and garnish to taste.

Alternative. Fold in 1 stiffly beaten egg white before turning the mixture into the mould.

EMMENTHAL MOUSSE

Suitable for a buffet party or for a light meal, with salad; or use in place of cheese at the end of a meal. It is best made with real

Emmenthal though one of the other cheeses will make a very good mousse.

QUANTITIES for 8 or more.

8 oz cheese (250 g)

Remove rind and cut the cheese in small pieces. Put in the goblet.

½ oz gelatine (1½ Tbs) dissolved in 4 Tbs hot water: ½ pt double cream (250 ml)

Add these to the cheese in the goblet and blend until quite smooth.

2 egg whites

Beat until stiff. Add the blended mixture and fold together carefully. Pour into a soufflé dish, or use individual dishes. Cool, cover and store in the refrigerator. Remove in time for it to come to room temperature for serving.

FISH MOUSSE

QUANTITIES for 4–5

½ oz gelatine (1½ Tbs): ¼ pt hot water (150 ml): 1 Tbs tarragon vinegar: Pinch paprika pepper

Put ingredients in the goblet and blend on slow speed for a few seconds or until the gelatine is dissolved.

8 oz cooked or canned fish, without bone (250 g)

Break up or flake the fish. If canned fish is used include all the contents of the can. Add fish to the goblet and blend until smooth.

¼ pt whipping cream (150 ml)

Open the top of the goblet and, with the motor running at high speed, pour in the cream. Mix for a few seconds. Taste for seasoning and pour into an oiled mould. Cool, cover and store in the refrigerator to set. Unmould and serve with salad and lemon wedges.

Alternative. Instead of all cream add half cream and half mayonnaise, adding the mayonnaise first and then the cream, both with the motor running.

HAM MOUSSE

QUANTITIES for 4 – 6

½ oz gelatine (1½ Tbs): 2 Tbs hot water

Dissolve the gelatine in the water.

8 oz lean cooked ham (250 g): 1 Tbs lemon juice: ¼ pt evaporated milk (150 ml): ½ tsp paprika pepper

Cut the ham in small pieces. Put half of it in the goblet with the milk, lemon juice and paprika. Blend until smooth. Empty into a bowl. If you have a large blender which will handle 8 oz meat in a thick mixture, there is no need to do the blending in two lots, simply add the remaining ingredients to the goblet.

¼ pt mayonnaise (150 ml)

Put the rest of the ham in the goblet with the mayonnaise and the dissolved gelatine and blend smooth. If done in two lots, combine the two.

1 egg white

Beat the egg until stiff and fold in the ham mixture. Pour into a 1½ pt mould which has been lightly oiled (½ l). Cover and put in the refrigerator to set.

Alternative. Line the mould with aspic jelly and allow this to set before pouring in the mousse. This gives a better appearance when the mousse is unmoulded.

CHEESE SOUFFLÉ

COOKING TIME: ½ hr. TEMPERATURE: E.375°F (190°C) G.5. QUANTITIES for 3 – 4 in a 1½ pt soufflé dish (¾ l).

½ oz butter (1 Tbs): 3 oz strong cheese (75 g): ½ oz flour (1½ Tbs): Pinch each of salt, mustard and pepper: ¼ pt hot milk (150 ml): 3 egg yolks

Cut the cheese in small pieces and put all ingredients in the blender goblet. Mix until smooth and pour back into the pan in which the milk was heated. Stir and cook over a low heat until smooth and thick. If it shows signs of becoming lumpy, stir vigorously and it will smooth out again.

3 egg whites

Beat until stiff enough to stand up in peaks. Fold into the cooked mixture and turn into the greased soufflé dish. Bake until risen and lightly browned.

FISH AND CHEESE SOUFFLÉ

COOKING TIME: 30 mins. TEMPERATURE: E.375°F (190°C) G.5.
QUANTITIES for 4

¼ pt cream (150 ml): 2 egg yolks: 8 oz cooked fish (250 g):
Salt and pepper: ¼ tsp paprika pepper

Remove all skin and bone and flake the fish. Put all the ingredients in the goblet and blend smooth.

2 egg whites

Beat until stiff and then add the fish mixture. Fold together. Put in a greased soufflé or baking dish.

Grated Parmesan cheese

Sprinkle the top with cheese (blended), and bake until risen and lightly browned. Serve plain or with a sauce such as mustard or Viennese Egg sauce: and with cucumber and tomato salad.

Alternative. Put the mixture in individual dishes and bake for 10 – 12 minutes.

HAM SOUFFLÉ

COOKING TIME: 30 mins. TEMPERATURE: E.375°F (190°C) G.5.
QUANTITIES for 3 – 4 or 1½ pt soufflé dish (¾ l). Grease the dish well.

4 oz lean, cooked ham (125 g)

Cut the meat in small pieces and blend to mince it finely. Tip into a basin.

1 oz butter or margarine (25 g): 1 oz flour (25 g): ¼ pt hot milk (150 ml): 3 egg yolks: ½ tsp dry mustard

Put in the goblet and blend until smooth. Return to the pan and stir vigorously until it forms a smooth, thick sauce. Simmer for 2 minutes. Add the ham and mix in. Add salt and pepper to taste.

3 egg whites

Beat the whites stiffly and fold them into the ham mixture. Turn into the prepared dish and bake until lightly browned, but still softish in the middle. Serve plain or with a

Parsley sauce.

SMOKED HADDOCK SOUFFLÉ

COOKING TIME: 30 – 35 mins. TEMPERATURE: E.375°F (190°C) G.5.

QUANTITIES for 3 – 4 or a 1½ pt soufflé dish (¾ l)

4 oz cooked smoked haddock (125 g)

Remove all bones and skin from the fish. Blend to shred finely and tip out.

1 oz butter or margarine (25 g): 1 oz flour (25 g): ¼ pt hot milk (150 ml): Pinch cayenne pepper: 3 egg yolks

Put ingredients in the goblet and blend smooth. Pour back into the pan used for heating the milk and stir and heat until it thickens. If it shows signs of becoming lumpy stir very hard and it will become smooth again. Cook for a minute. Mix in the haddock.

3 egg whites

Beat until stiff enough to stand up in peaks and fold into the sauce mixture. Put in the greased soufflé dish and bake until well risen and lightly browned. Serve with a sauce such as parsley or mustard sauce.

Chapter Ten

SAVOURY FLANS, QUICHES AND PASTIES

In modern menus these have largely taken the place of the more substantial double-crust tarts and pies of the past.

A supply of pastry cases can be kept ready in the freezer and making a filling is a matter of a few minutes' preparation with the blender.

CHICKEN AND HAM TURNOVERS

COOKING TIME: 25 – 30 mins. TEMPERATURE: E.450°F (230°C) G.8.

QUANTITIES for 4 large turnovers

½ pt hot milk or chicken stock (250 ml): 1 oz butter or margarine (25 g): 1 oz flour (25 g)

Put ingredients in the goblet and blend until smooth. Heat in a pan, stirring until the sauce boils, simmer for 3 minutes, stirring occasionally. Put aside to become cold.

4 oz cooked chicken meat (125 g): 4 oz cooked ham (125 g)
Salt and pepper: Ground mace or nutmeg

Cut the meat in small pieces removing any fat, gristle, skin or bone. Blend in two or more lots until it is finely minced, using the on/off technique at slow speed and scraping down as necessary. Tip each lot into a bowl. Add the cold sauce and season with salt and pepper and the mace or nutmeg.

12 oz puff pastry (375 g)

Roll the pastry into an oblong not more than an eighth of an inch thick (3 mm). Cut into four pieces and put some of the meat mixture on half of each piece. Moisten the edges of the pastry with water or milk, fold in half and seal. Put on a baking tray, brush with egg and water, or with milk and cut a small slit in the top of each turnover. Bake until the pastry is crisp and brown. Serve hot or cold, with salad.

COTTAGE CHEESE AND HAM QUICHE

COOKING TIME: 30 mins. TEMPERATURE: E.425°F (220°C) G.7.
QUANTITIES for 7 – 8 in. (18 – 20 cm) flan

Line the flan ring with short pastry and prick the bottom with a fork. Put in the refrigerator to chill.

3 oz strong cheese (75 g)

Cut in small pieces and blend to grate finely. Set aside one ounce for putting on top of the filling. Put the rest in a bowl.

3 oz cooked ham or fried bacon, cut up (75 g)

Blend until finely shredded and put in the bowl with the cheese.

2 eggs: 4 Tbs milk or cream: 8 oz cottage cheese (250 g): Salt and pepper

Put in the goblet and blend until smooth. Add to the ham and cheese and mix well. Pour into the flan case and sprinkle the remaining cheese over the top. Bake until lightly browned. Serve hot or cold.

FRENCH CHEESE TART

COOKING TIME: 25 mins. TEMPERATURE: E.400°F (200°C) G.6.
QUANTITIES for an 8 in. (20 cm) tart

Short pastry

Line a flan ring or pie plate with the pastry and chill it in the refrigerator.

2 eggs: Grated nutmeg: ¼ pt single cream (150 ml): Pinch cayenne pepper: 4 oz Emmenthal cheese (125 g)

Cut the cheese in pieces and put all the ingredients in the blender goblet and mix until smooth. Pour into the pastry shell and bake until the pastry is lightly coloured and the filling firm and brown. Serve hot or cold.
Variation. Fry a small chopped onion in a little fat and strew it over the bottom of the pastry before adding the filling.

FRIED MEAT PASTIES

A popular way of using up small amounts of left-over meat or poultry.

COOKING TIME: about 10 mins. QUANTITIES for 5 – 6 pasties
Short crust pastry using 4 oz flour (125 g)

Roll the pastry very thinly, the thinner the better. Cut it into approximately 5 inch (12 cm) squares.

2 – 3 oz cooked meat (50 – 75 g): 2 – 3 oz cooked spinach or other left-over vegetables (50 – 75 g): ¼ pt gravy or sauce (150 ml): Pinch of dried garlic: 1 tsp Soya or Worcester sauce: Salt and pepper

Remove fat, skin and gristle from the meat, cut in pieces and blend on slow speed to shred it finely. Tip into a bowl. Blend the other ingredients until well mixed and combine them with the meat. Put a little of the mixture on each piece of pastry, moisten the edges and fold over, pressing very firmly to seal them. Fry them in a little hot oil or fat, in a frying pan, until they are brown on both sides. They are nicer if the minimum amount of fat is used, just enough to prevent sticking. Serve hot with Gravy or other savoury sauce.

FORCEMEAT PASTIES

These are made by rolling puff pastry very thinly, cutting into rounds which are stuck together in pairs with the filling in between. Fry in the same way as above.

KIPPER QUICHE

COOKING TIME: 35 mins. TEMPERATURE: E.425°F (200°C) G.4. QUANTITIES for a 7 in. flan (18 cm)

Shorty pastry using 4 oz flour (125 g)

Roll the pastry and line the flan. Put in the refrigerator while making the filling.

8 oz kipper fillets (250 g) or 1 lb kippers on the bone (500 g)

Put the kippers in a heat resistant jug or basin and pour boiling water over them. Cover and leave for 10 minutes. Drain, remove all skin and bone and flake the fish. Put it in the flan case.

2 oz hard cheese (50 g)

Cut in pieces and blend to grate. Tip out and set aside.

1 egg: 4 Tbs milk or cream: 1 Tbs French mustard: Pinch of cayenne pepper

Blend to beat the egg and mix the ingredients. Pour over the kippers and sprinkle the cheese on top. Bake until the filling is set. Serve hot or cold.

Alternative. Add a few stoned black olives after sprinkling on the cheese.

LAMB FLAN
(for using up the last of the joint)

COOKING TIME: 35 mins. TEMPERATURE: E.450°F (230°C) G.8. QUANTITIES for a 7 in. (18 cm) flan

Line the flan case with short crust pastry.

8 oz lean cooked lamb (250 g): 2 oz grilled or fried bacon (50 g)

Remove any skin or gristle from the lamb and cut it and the bacon in small pieces. Blend the meat to shred it, doing this in one or more lots according to the size of the blender. Tip into a basin.

*1 can condensed vegetable soup 10½ oz (198 g): A little mint
sauce or some Worcester sauce: Pepper*

Add to the meat and mix well. Spread evenly in the flan case and
bake until the pastry is lightly browned.

Chopped parsley or sliced tomato

Serve hot with a parsley or tomato garnish.

Alternative. If there are any pastry trimmings to spare use these to
make a lattice top or cut in small circles or other shapes and put
on top of the meat before baking.

ONION AND EGG FLAN

COOKING TIME: 40 mins. TEMPERATURE: E.400°F (200°C) G.6.
QUANTITIES for a 7 in. (18 cm) flan

Line the flan with short crust pastry, prick the base with a fork and
put the flan in the refrigerator while the filling is made.

8 oz onions (250 g): 1 oz butter or margarine (25 g)

Skin and cut the onions in quarters. Put in the goblet, cover with
cold water and blend on/off just to chop them. Strain and press
out the moisture. Melt the fat and stew the onions in it over a low
heat until they are tender but not brown. Cool a little and return
to the goblet.

*2 eggs: 4 Tbs cream: Salt and pepper: Nutmeg or mace: Pinch
of sugar*

Add to the goblet and blend until the mixture is smooth. Pour
into the flan case and cook until the pastry is lightly browned
and the filling set. Serve warm or cold.

QUICHE LORRAINE

COOKING TIME: 45 – 50 mins. TEMPERATURE: E.425°F (220°C)
G.7. for the pastry, then E.350°F (150°C) G.4. for the filling.
QUANTITIES for a 7 – 8 in. (18 – 20 cm) flan

6 oz short pastry (150 g)

Roll out pastry and line the flan. Line it with a piece of foil and
bake until the pastry is set but not completely cooked. Remove
the foil.

3 – 4 rashers of bacon

Remove rinds and grill or fry the bacon. Cut it in small pieces and put them in the bottom of the flan.

¼ pt milk (150 ml): 2 Tbs cream: 2 eggs: ¼ tsp dry mustard: ½ tsp salt: 3 oz well-flavoured cheese (75 g): Pinch pepper

Cut the cheese in pieces and blend all the ingredients together until smooth. Pour over the bacon. Bake until the filling is set and lightly browned. Serve warm or cold.

SAGE AND ONION QUICHE

COOKING TIME: 40 mins. TEMPERATURE: E.400°F (200°C) G.6. QUANTITIES for a 7 in. (18 cm) flan

Line the flan with short crust pastry, prick the bottom with a fork and put it in the refrigerator.

¼ pt milk (150 ml): 1 egg: A small onion, cut in half: 3 oz well-flavoured cheese (75 g): Salt and pepper: 3 fresh sage leaves, or more to taste

Cut the cheese in pieces and put all the ingredients in the goblet. Blend until the sage is chopped finely and the cheese is grated. Pour into the pastry case and cook until the filling is set and lightly browned. Serve warm or cold.

SMOKED HADDOCK PIE

COOKING TIME: about 15 mins. for the filling; 30 mins. for the pie. The filling is best prepared in advance.

TEMPERATURE: E.425°F (220°C) G.7. QUANTITIES for 4

1 lb smoked haddock fillets (500 g): ½ pt milk (250 ml)

Poach the fish in the milk for about 10 minutes, drain, keeping the milk. Make the milk up to ½ pt with water.

4 oz lean bacon rashers (125 g): 1 oz butter or margarine (25 g): 2 Tbs flour: 1 sprig parsley: 1 tsp dry mustard

Remove rinds and cut the bacon in pieces. Blend with the milk, fat, flour and flavourings to chop the bacon and parsley. Put in a pan and stir until it boils, boil 1 – 2 minutes. Remove all skin and bones from the fish and put the flakes in the sauce.

1 hard boiled egg

Shell and cut up roughly. Add to the sauce.

1 tsp lemon juice: Pepper

Season the mixture to taste and put it in a 1½ pt (1 l) piedish with a pie funnel in the middle. The funnel is advisable because something is needed to hold the pastry up. It is not advisable to fill the piedish to the top with the fish mixture as it will then boil over. If possible leave the pie to cool before covering.

8 oz puff pastry (250 g): Milk or egg for brushing

Roll the pastry very thinly. Cut strips for the edge of the dish. Stick them on with milk or egg, brushing the top side with liquid too. Put on the main piece of pastry. Cut a hole in the centre, decorate with pastry trimmings, brush with milk or egg and bake until the pastry is brown and well risen. Serve hot.

SWISS SPINACH TART

COOKING TIME: 45 – 50 mins. TEMPERATURE: E.425°F (220°C) G.7.
QUANTITIES for an 8 in. flan (20 cm)

Short pastry using 4 – 6 oz flour (125 – 150 g)

Roll the pastry and line the flan. Prick the bottom well and bake blind for 15 minutes, see Quiche Lorraine, page 78.

8 oz cooked or canned spinach (250 g): 5 Tbs cream or evaporated milk (75 ml): 2 eggs: Salt and Pepper: Ground mace or nutmeg

Blend together until smooth. Pour into the baked pastry case.

2 oz diced bacon (50 g)

Sprinkle the bacon over the top of the filling and bake for 30 minutes or until the filling is set. Serve hot.

Alternative. Sprinkle the top with grated cheese as well as the bacon.

Chapter Eleven

FISH BALLS, CROQUETTES, MOULDS, MOUSSELINES AND QUENELLES

Many recipes made with pulped or sieved raw fish which used to be very complicated and messy to make, are easy with a blender. Recipes using cooked and canned fish are also much easier to make with the use of a blender.

Raw or cooked fish can be blended without added ingredients if required thus for the recipe. Be very careful to remove all skin and bones as these would interfere with the action of the cutting blades of the blender, the exception to this being canned fish where skin and bones are soft and will blend perfectly with the flesh of the fish.

For a very smooth blend use some liquid, not less than ¼ pt (150 ml) of liquid per 8 oz (250 g) of fish.

FISH, CHEESE AND ALMOND CROQUETTES

COOKING TIME: 15 mins. QUANTITIES *for 4 croquettes*

1 oz bread (25 g)

Remove crusts, break bread up small and blend to fine crumbs. Put on a piece of greaseproof paper and set aside for coating the croquettes.

1 oz blanched almonds (25 g): 2 oz hard cheese (50 g)

Blend separately or together on slow speed to chop the nuts and grate the cheese. Put in a mixing bowl.

8 oz cooked white fish fillets (250 g)

This represents about 12 oz (375 g) of raw fish. Remove any skin and bones and flake the fish or blend it. Add to the nuts and cheese.

2 oz onion (50 g): 2 Tbs oil

Blend the onion on/off to chop it. Fry it brown in the hot oil. Add to the fish and mix well.

81

Salt and pepper: 1 egg

Add seasoning to the fish mixture. Beat the egg a little and use enough to bind the fish mixture but avoid making it sloppy. Mix the remaining egg with a little water and pour it in a flat dish. Shape the mixture into four flat cakes, coat them in flour, then in egg and then in the crumbs, patting well to make them stick. Fry the croquettes slowly in shallow hot oil until the outsides are brown and crisp.

FISH MOUSSELINE

COOKING TIME: 40 mins. TEMPERATURE: E.400°F (200°C) G.6. QUANTITIES for 4

12 oz raw fillets of white fish (375 g): 3 egg whites: 1 tsp salt: 8 oz double cream (250 ml): Pinch of pepper

Remove all skin and bone from the fish and cut it in strips. Do the blending in one or two lots depending on the capacity of the machine. Blend all the ingredients together until smooth. Mix the lots afterwards. Spread the mixture evenly in a well-greased border mould and stand the mould in a pan of hot water. Bake until the mousseline is set. Remove the mould from the water and allow it to stand for at least 5 minutes to settle before turning it out on a hot dish.

Cooked peas, mushrooms or other vegetables: A sauce such as Hollandaise, Green Dutch, Fish Velouté or any other fish sauce

Pile the vegetables in the centre of the mould and either pour the sauce over the mould or serve it separately.

FISH SHAPE
(using cooked fish)

COOKING TIME: 1¼ – 1½ hrs. QUANTITIES for 4

2 oz white bread, without crusts (50 g)

Tear the bread in pieces and feed it through the top of the goblet with the motor running at slow speed. Blend to make fine crumbs and tip into a mixing bowl.

2 oz melted butter or margarine (50 g): 6 Tbs milk: Small strip of lemon rind: 3 eggs: Salt and pepper: Mace or nutmeg

Put in the goblet and blend together thoroughly.

12 oz cooked, flaked white fish (375 g)

Have the fish warm or at room temperature and be sure all skin and bones have been removed. Add to the liquid in the goblet and blend to mash the fish well. Pour into a greased basin or mould, 1½ pt size (1 l). Cover with a lid of foil and steam until set. Unmould on a hot dish and mask with a sauce such as

Parsley, tomato, anchovy, green Dutch, or pimento sauce.

NORWEGIAN FISH MOULD
(using raw fish)

COOKING TIME: 1 hr. TEMPERATURE: E.400°F (200°C) G.6. QUANTITIES for 4 – 6

1 lb white fish fillets (500 g): 1 tsp salt: Pinch pepper: ½ pt milk (250 ml): 1½ Tbs potato flour or cornflour: ¼ pt cream (150 ml)

Remove any skin and bones and cut the fish in strips. Blend the ingredients together in two or more lots, putting some of the liquid in the goblet first and then the fish. Blend until the fish is well broken up. Tip into a basin and finally mix the lot together. Put the mixture in a well-oiled ring mould or baking dish, 1½ pt size (1 l). Stand the dish in a baking tin of hot water and bake until set. Remove from the water and stand for a few minutes before turning out on a hot serving dish. Serve with a well-coloured and flavoured sauce such as

Hollandaise, anchovy or tomato sauce.

NORWEGIAN FISH BALLS

Proceed in the same way as for quenelles but use the palms of the hands to roll the mixture into small balls. These may then be poached or fried. Tiny ones are used to garnish fish soups, larger ones as a dish on their own with a suitable sauce, for example, tomato, anchovy, pimento or cheese sauce.

QUENELLES

COOKING TIME: 10 mins. QUANTITIES for 12 quenelles

8 oz white fish fillets (150 g): ½ tsp salt: Pinch of pepper: ¼ pt milk (150 ml): 1 Tbs potato flour or cornflour: 5 Tbs cream

Remove all skin and bone from the raw fillets and cut the fish in strips. Blend all the ingredients together in one or more lots depending on the capacity of the blender. Process until the fish is well broken up. Put in a basin, cover and leave in the refrigerator for at least an hour for the mixture to become firm. To shape the quenelles use two tablespoons. Fill one and smooth the piled up top with a knife. Dip the second spoon in boiling water and press it over the mixture in the other spoon. Rotate gently to make an even shape. Drop the quenelles into boiling water and poach for 10 minutes. Drain and serve as a garnish for another fish dish or by themselves with a sauce, such as hollandaise.

SALMON OR TUNA LOAF

COOKING TIME: 45 mins. TEMPERATURE: E.350°F (180°C) G.4. QUANTITIES for 4 – 6

3 oz bread (75 g)

Remove crusts, break bread in small pieces and feed through the top of the blender goblet with the motor running at slow speed. Blend to fine crumbs. Tip into a mixing bowl.

¼ pt milk (150 ml): 8 oz canned salmon or tuna (250 g): 2 eggs: Pinch of pepper: 1 tsp salt: 1 Tbs lemon juice

Put these in the goblet, including liquid and bones in the can. Blend smooth and mix with the crumbs. Put in a well-oiled 1 lb size (½ kg) loaf pan and bake until set. To serve hot, turn out on a hot dish and mask with

Parsley, anchovy, tomato or hollandaise sauce

To serve cold, store in the tin in which it was baked. Unmould and cut in slices. Garnish with salad.

SPANISH FISH BALLS
(using cooked fish)

COOKING TIME: about 10 mins. QUANTITIES for 4 – 5

1 lb cooked fish (500 g)

Remove skin and bones from the fish and either break it up into flakes or put in the blender to mince. Tip into a bowl.

2 oz bread (50 g)

Break into small pieces and blend on slow speed to make fine crumbs. Add to the fish.

2 eggs: 2 oz cheese cut up (50 g): 2 sprigs parsley: ¼ tsp dried garlic or ½ a fresh clove: Salt and pepper

Put in the goblet and blend to grate the cheese and chop the parsley. Add to the fish mixture and combine thoroughly. Shape into 24 small balls. Fry brown in shallow or deep fat or oil. Serve with a good fish sauce.

Chapter Twelve

BAKED FISH

FISH WITH AUBERGINE SAUCE

COOKING TIME: 30 mins. TEMPERATURE: E.375°F (190°C) G.5.
QUANTITIES for 4

8 oz aubergine (250 g)

Wash, remove the stalk and cut in pieces for the blender. Cover with cold water and blend just enough to chop the aubergine in small pieces. Strain and put in a pan.

2 Tbs olive oil: 2 Tbs tomato paste: 2 canned red pimentos: Pinch dried garlic or some fresh

Put in the goblet and blend until smooth. Add to the aubergine and simmer for 10 minutes. Season to taste with salt and pepper and add a little water as needed during cooking but not to make it sloppy.

4 portions white fish fillets

Put the fish in an oiled baking dish, cover with the sauce and bake until the fish is cooked, about 20 minutes.

Alternative. Sprinkle the sauce with a gratin of dried breadcrumbs mixed with grated cheese and then bake.

AUBERGINE SAUCE WITH GRILLED OR FRIED FISH

Simmer the sauce for 20 – 30 minutes, adding water as needed and serve it as an accompaniment to grilled or fried white fish.

FISH WITH CHEESE TOPPING

COOKING TIME: 25 – 30 mins. TEMPERATURE: E.400°F (200°C) G.6.
QUANTITIES for 4

4 cutlets or fillets of white fish

Put in a single layer in a greased baking dish.

1 small onion: 1 oz butter or margarine (25 g)

Slice the onion or chop it in the blender. Fry it brown in the hot fat.

1 oz bread (25 g): 2 oz cheese (50 g)

Break the bread in small pieces and cut up the cheese. Blend these together on slow speed until finely grated. Tip out and add the onions, a teaspoon of salt and a pinch of pepper. Put the mixture on top of the fish and bake. Serve with

Lemon wedges.

Alternative. Moisten the bottom of the dish with ¼ pt (150 ml) dry white wine and then bake.

FISH CRÉOLE

COOKING TIME: 20 mins. TEMPERATURE: E.375°F (190°C) G.5.
QUANTITIES for 4

2 oz bread and butter or margarine (50 g)

Cut the bread in pieces and blend it to make buttered crumbs. Tip into a small bowl.

1½ lb fillets white fish (750 g)

Cut in portions and put in a shallow oiled baking dish, in a single layer if possible. Sprinkle with salt and pepper.

4 oz onion (125 g): 1 oz fat (25 g) or 2 Tbs oil

Skin the onion and cut it in pieces. Blend to chop it and then fry it in the hot fat or oil. Return to the goblet.

2 oz green pepper (50 g): 8 oz tomatoes, fresh or canned (250 g); 4 oz mushrooms (125 g): Salt and pepper

Remove seeds and slice the peppers, wash and slice the mushrooms, wash and cut up the tomatoes. Add to the onions in the goblet and blend to a smooth sauce. Pour over the fish to coat it. Sprinkle the breadcrumbs on top and bake near the top of the oven until the fish is tender and the topping lightly browned. If necessary, this can be browned at the end under the grill.

FISH FILLETS AU GRATIN

COOKING TIME: 15 – 20 mins. TEMPERATURE: E.425°F (220°C) G.7.
QUANTITIES for 4

3 oz bread (75 g): ½ oz butter or margarine (1 Tbs)

Break the bread in pieces and feed it through the top of the goblet with the motor running at slow speed. Blend to fine crumbs. Heat the fat and dry the crumbs brown. Set aside.

4 oz mushrooms (125 g): 1 – 2 slices onion: 1 sprig parsley: 2 Tbs water: Yellow rind of ½ lemon or 1 Tbs juice

Blend together to chop the onion and mushrooms. Put half the mixture in a shallow, greased baking dish large enough to take

4 portions of white fish fillets.

Sprinkle a tablespoon of crumbs over the layer of vegetables. Put the fish on top. Sprinkle it with salt and pepper and put the rest of the mushroom mixture on top of the fish.

¼ pt dry white wine or fish stock (150 ml): 1 oz butter or margarine (25 g)

Pour the liquid carefully round the fish using just enough to moisten the vegetable layer. Sprinkle the fish with the remaining crumbs and dot with the butter or margarine. Bake.

STUFFED FILLETS OF PLAICE OR SOLE

COOKING TIME: 20 mins. TEMPERATURE: E.375°F (190°C) G.5.
QUANTITIES for 4

1 oz bread (25 g): 1 strip yellow lemon rind

Break up the bread and put it in the goblet with the lemon. Blend
on slow speed to crumb the bread and grate the lemon. Tip into
a basin.

6 oz tomatoes (150 g): 2 oz mushrooms (50 g): Salt and pepper

Put in the goblet and blend to a pulp. Add to the breadcrumbs
and mix well.

*1 lb fillets plaice or sole (500 g): About ½ pt fish stock, wine or
cider (250 ml): 2 oz chopped mushrooms (50 g)*

Spread the stuffing mixture on the fillets. Roll them up tightly and
pack them close together in a casserole or baking dish. Sprinkle
the chopped mushrooms on top and pour enough liquid round
the sides to moisten well. Cover the dish with a lid and bake.

Chapter Thirteen

MEAT FRICADELLES, MOULDS, CROQUETTES, BURGERS AND PUDDINGS

Mincing or shredding cooked meat is much quicker in the blender
than in a mincing machine and frequently the other ingredients
can be blended with the meat to give a good flavour distribution.

Other recipes using cooked meat will be found in the sections
on Pâtés and Spreads; Batters; Soufflés and Mousses; and
Savoury Flans and Quiches.

BEEF FRICADELLES

COOKING TIME: 10 – 15 mins. QUANTITIES for 4

8 oz cold cooked beef (250 g)

Remove any gristle or skin and cut the meat in small pieces.
Blend in one or two lots to shred it finely. Tip into a bowl.

4 oz mashed potato (125 g)

If ready mashed potato is not to hand use mashed potato powder instead. Make 1 oz (25 g) of the powder with ¼ pt (150 ml) milk and water. Allow it to become cold before mixing it with the meat.

1 oz onion (25 g): Salt and pepper: Grated nutmeg: 1 egg

Blend together to chop the onion and use it to mix the meat and potatoes. If any more liquid seems to be needed to moisten the mixture use a little wine or bottled sauce. It should be soft enough to mould easily. Turn the mixture onto a floured board and divide into four pieces. Shape each into a large round flat cake. Fry slowly in hot oil or butter until well browned on both sides. Serve hot with a well-flavoured gravy or sauce and a green salad.

CHICKEN AND HAM MOULD

QUANTITIES for 4 – 6

½ pt chicken stock (250 ml): ½ oz gelatine (1½ Tbs)

Heat the stock and dissolve the gelatine in it. Pour a little into the bottom of a 1 pint (½ l) mould and leave to set.

8 oz cooked chicken and ham, mixed (250 g)

Cut the meat in small pieces, removing all skin and gristle. Blend on slow speed to shred it. Tip into a bowl.

⅛ pt of tarragon leaves (60 ml): Grated nutmeg or mace: 1 tsp Worcester sauce: Salt and pepper

Blend the tarragon leaves with water to cover, until finely chopped. Strain and add to the meat, the rest of the stock and the seasonings.

1 hard boiled egg

Shell and slice and use to decorate the jelly set at the bottom of the mould. Carefully add the chicken mixture and leave until set. Turn out and serve with salad.

CHICKEN OR RABBIT TIMBALES

COOKING TIME: 30 mins. TEMPERATURE: E.350°F (180°C) G.4.
QUANTITIES for three 8 oz pudding moulds (200 ml) or 4 – 6 timbale moulds

1 oz butter or margarine (25 g): 1 oz bread (25 g): 2 sprigs parsley or tarragon: 2 eggs: 1 tsp salt: Pepper: ¼ pt hot stock (150 ml): 6 oz cooked chicken or rabbit (150 g)

Cut the fat in small pieces and break up the bread. Cut the chicken or rabbit in small pieces. Blend all ingredients together in one or two lots, until smooth. Mix the lots and pour into well-oiled moulds. I use the 8 oz pudding moulds but the smaller timbales can be used. Stand the moulds in a pan of hot water and bake until firm. Remove from the water and stand a few minutes to allow them to settle. Turn out on a hot dish and serve with a well-flavoured sauce.

CHICKEN OR TURKEY CROQUETTES

COOKING TIME: 2 – 3 mins. to fry. Advance preparation necessary.

QUANTITIES for 8 croquettes

2 – 3 oz stale bread (50 – 75 g)

Tear the bread in pieces and blend it to fine crumbs. Tip into a flat dish.

10 oz cooked chicken or turkey, without bone (300 g)

Remove all skin and gristle and cut the meat in small pieces. Blend it on slow speed, on/off, in two or three lots, until it is finely minced. Tip into a basin.

1 oz butter or margarine (25 g): 1 oz flour (25 g): 1 slice o onion: 8 oz hot stock or milk (250 ml): ½ tsp salt: Pinch o pepper

Blend these together until smooth.

2 sprigs parsley: 1 oz sliced mushrooms (25 g)

Add to the goblet and blend just enough to chop them. Pour into a pan and stir until it boils, boil 2 – 3 minutes. Add the meat and boil a further 2 – 3 minutes. Tip out on a large dish and put to cool, then refrigerate until firm. Divide the mixture into 8 pieces and roll each into a cylinder, using a little flour for rolling it in.

Beaten egg and water

Roll the croquettes in egg to coat them well and then in the bread-crumbs, and pat to make them stick.

90

Frying oil: Piquante sauce such as Salsa Verde, page 51

Fry the croquettes in hot oil until they are brown. Drain on absorbent paper and keep hot. Serve with a piquante sauce.

FRIED BEEF CAKES

COOKING TIME: 10 mins. QUANTITIES for 4 cakes

2 oz bread (50 g)

Tear the bread in pieces and blend it at slow speed to make fine crumbs. Put in a bowl.

4 oz cooked beef (125 g)

Remove skin and gristle and cut in small pieces. Blend at slow speed in one or two lots to shred it finely. Add to the crumbs.

Salt and pepper: 1 egg: 3 Tbs wine or stock: ½ tsp paprika pepper: Shake of garlic salt

Blend to beat the egg and mix the flavourings. Add to the meat and combine well. Divide into four, and shape into flat cakes. Fry brown on both sides in a little hot oil.

Alternative flavourings
1. Blend a strip of lemon rind or some fresh herbs with the crumbs.
2. Add a small piece of cheese to the crumbs when blending.
3. Add some cooked ham to the beef.

MEAT BURGERS

COOKING TIME: 10 – 15 mins. QUANTITIES for 4 burgers

8 oz cold cooked meat (250 g)

Remove fat and gristle and cut the meat in small pieces. Blend at slow speed to shred it. Tip into a basin.

1 small onion: 2 sprigs parsley

Peel and halve the onion and put it in the goblet with the parsley and cold water to cover. Blend to chop, drain, and add to the meat.

Pepper: 2 tsp flour: Egg to bind (about ½)

Add to the meat mixture using enough egg to bind. Shape into round cakes about 1 inch (2 cm) thick.

4 rashers streaky bacon

Remove rinds and wrap a rasher round each meat burger, fastening with a cocktail stick. Fry in shallow fat or grill until brown on both sides. Serve hot with

Sauce or gravy: Vegetable purée or salad.

STEAMED MEAT PUDDING
(using raw minced meat)

COOKING TIME: 1 hr. QUANTITIES for 6 – 8

Thoroughly grease a 1½ – 2 pint basin (1 l). Dust it with fine dried breadcrumbs. If you have none at hand, blend a couple of dry biscuits to fine crumbs.

1 lb raw minced meat, any kind (500 g)

Put in a mixing bowl and break up with a spoon.

2 oz streaky bacon (50 g): ¼ pt milk (150 ml): 3 eggs: A strip of yellow lemon rind: 1 tsp brandy: Salt and pepper

Remove the rind and any bones from the bacon. Cut it in small pieces and put it in the goblet with the other ingredients. Blend until smooth, add to the meat and combine well. Put in the prepared basin, cover with a lid of foil and steam. Leave to stand for 5 minutes before turning out on a hot dish. Mask with a

Brown sauce or tomato sauce.

Chapter Fourteen

MEAT CASSEROLES

With many casserole recipes the vegetables, herbs and flavourings can be blended to a smooth sauce before cooking. Alternatively, use the blender for chopping the onion and other vegetables required for the casserole.

When meat has been braised with vegetables round it, blend the vegetables with the cooking liquid, to make a rich, smooth sauce to serve with the meat. Check the seasoning at this stage. Wine or cream can be added then, too.

BEEF CASSEROLE

COOKING TIME: 2 – 3 hrs. TEMPERATURE: E.325°F (160°C) G.3. QUANTITIES for 4

1 lb stewing steak (500 g): 1 tsp salt: 2 Tbs flour: Pinch of pepper: 1 oz lard (25 g)

Cut the meat in pieces and coat it in the flour and seasonings. Heat the lard and fry the meat brown. Put it in the casserole.

8 oz carrots (250 g): 2 medium onions

Prepare and cut in rough pieces.

Pinch dried garlic: 1 beef cube: Pinch thyme: ¼ pt red wine (150 ml): 1 sprig parsley

Blend these with half the carrots, the onions, and water to cover. Blend until smooth. Pour over the meat. Blend the remaining carrots to chop coarsely and add to the meat. Cover and cook gently until the meat is tender. For extra flavour, add a bay leaf, removing it before serving.

BRAISED BEEF

COOKING TIME: 2 hrs. TEMPERATURE: E.350°F (180°C) G.4. QUANTITIES for 6

1½ – 2 lb topside of beef or other lean cut (1 kg): Oil or chopped beef fat

Trim any fat from the meat, cut small and heat in a pan until the fat runs. Use this, or hot oil, for browning the meat well on all sides.

1 oz diced bacon (25 g): 5 Tbs red wine: Small piece of green pepper, diced: Bouquet garni: 1 onion, sliced: ½ tsp salt: 2 oz sliced mushrooms (50 g)

Remove meat from pan and drain off the fat. Put in the bacon and other ingredients and return the meat. Cover and cook gently

93

until the meat is tender, turning it once. Remove meat and slice it. Remove the bouquet garni and blend the vegetables and stock to make a smooth sauce. Add gravy browning if a darker sauce is wanted. Pour the sauce over the meat or serve separately.

BEEF AND MUSHROOM CASSEROLE

COOKING TIME: 2 – 3 hrs. TEMPERATURE: E. 325 – 350°F (160 – 180°C) G.3 – 4. QUANTITIES for 4

1 lb stewing or braising steak cut in 4 pieces (500 g): 3 oz streaky bacon cut in pieces (75 g)

Fry the bacon gently until it is crisp. Lift out with a perforated spoon or ladle and put it in the blender goblet. Brown the meat in the bacon fat and put it in the casserole.

¼ pt red wine (150 ml): ¼ pt canned consommé (150 ml): 2 tsp dry mustard: 1 Tbs flour: ½ tsp salt: Pinch of pepper: 1 small onion cut in half: 2 oz mushrooms (50 g), sliced

Put in the goblet with the bacon and blend until smooth. Pour into the frying pan and stir until boiling, scraping the sediment from the bottom of the pan as you stir. Pour over the steak.

Bouquet garni

Add to the casserole, cover and cook slowly until the meat is tender. Remove the bouquet garni and serve.

BEEF OLIVES

COOKING TIME: 1½ – 2 hrs. TEMPERATURE: E.350°F (180°C) G.4. QUANTITIES for 4

2 oz bread (50 g): 2 oz prepared suet (50 g)

Break the bread in pieces and blend it to fine crumbs. Put in a basin with the suet.

1 egg: Pinch of ground mace or nutmeg: 1 tsp dried thyme: 2 sprigs parsley: ½ tsp salt: Pinch of pepper: Thin strip of lemon rind

Blend these together until the parsley and lemon are chopped finely. Add to the crumbs and suet with enough milk to bind.

1 lb topside or rump steak (500 g) cut in thin slices of about 4 oz each (125 g)

Spread each piece of meat with some of the stuffing. Roll up and secure with white cotton or wooden cocktail sticks.

1 oz fat (25 g)

Brown the meat rolls in this.

1 onion cut up: 1 carrot cut up: ½ tsp salt: Pinch of pepper: 1 Tbs flour: ½ pt stock (250 ml)

Blend smooth. Pour over the olives, cover and cook until tender.

CHICKEN CASSEROLE

When cooked, the chicken has the colour of fried chicken, but no high-calorie fat has been used.

COOKING TIME: 1½ hrs. TEMPERATURE: E.350°F (180°C) G.4. QUANTITIES for 4

4 portions of chicken

Wash and put in a casserole, preferably in a single layer.

1 Tbs capers: 2 oz stuffed olives (50 g): 1 tsp salt

Sprinkle over the chicken.

8 oz canned tomatoes: 1 green pepper: 1 onion

Remove the seeds from the pepper and cut it in pieces. Skin the onion and cut in pieces. Put both in the goblet with the tomatoes and blend to chop the vegetables finely. Pour over the chicken and add water almost to cover. Cook gently until the chicken is tender. Any surplus liquid will be good in a soup.

CHICKEN WITH GREEN PEPPERS

COOKING TIME: 1 hr. or more. TEMPERATURE: E.350°F (180°C) G.4. QUANTITIES for 4

4 chicken joints: 1 oz butter (25 g)

Heat the butter and fry the chicken until brown.

2 sliced green peppers: 2 oz onion (50 g)

Skin and cut the onion in pieces. Put the vegetables in the goblet with cold water to cover. Blend just long enough, on slow speed, to chop the vegetables small. Strain and add to the chicken, cooking for a few minutes longer.

¼ pt stock (150 ml): ¼ pt double cream or evaporated milk (150 ml): Salt and pepper

Add to the chicken. If the frying was not done in the casserole, transfer the chicken and sauce to a casserole, cover and cook until the chicken is tender. Serve the chicken on a hot dish with the sauce which may be left as it is or blended to make it smooth.

CHICKEN WITH GREEN TARRAGON SAUCE

COOKING TIME: 1 – 1½ hrs. TEMPERATURE: E.350°F (180°C) G.4.
QUANTITIES for 4

4 portions chicken: 2 Tbs oil

Fry chicken brown in the hot oil.

½ pt milk (250 ml): 3 Tbs white wine: 2 Tbs cornflour: ⅛ pt fresh tarragon leaves (75 ml): Pinch fresh or dried thyme: 1 tsp salt: Pinch pepper

Blend all together until the tarragon is finely chopped. Put the pieces of chicken in a casserole and drain off surplus oil from the frying pan. Pour in the blended sauce and stir until it boils. Pour it over the chicken, cover, and cook in the oven until the chicken is tender.

LAMB CUTLETS IN YOGURT SAUCE

COOKING TIME: 30 – 40 mins. TEMPERATURE: E.375°F (190°C) G.5.
QUANTITIES for 4 – 6

2 lb best end of neck cutlets (1 kg): 1 oz fat or oil (25 g)

Trim the cutlets and fry them slowly in the fat or oil. If possible do this in a large, shallow sauté pan or casserole. Failing that, fry them in a frying pan and transfer them to a casserole for the final cooking. If you want the sauce to remain white, do not allow the cutlets to brown. Give them about 5 minutes each side.

4 oz onion (125 g)

Peel the onion and cut in pieces. Either blend dry or covered with cold water, giving just a second or so to chop finely. Strain if done in water and press out surplus water. Remove the cutlets and fry the onions in the same fat for 3 – 4 minutes. If the cooking is to be finished in a casserole transfer the onion to it. Season with salt and pepper and put the cutlets on top.

White wine: A bay leaf

Add enough white wine to moisten the layer of onions and add the bay leaf. Cover and cook until the meat is tender. Lift out and keep hot.

½ pt yogurt (250 ml): 2 tsp potato flour

Put the onions and juices in the goblet with the yogurt and potato flour and blend smooth. Put in a pan or return to the cooking dish and stir until the sauce thickens and just comes to the boil. Serve with the cutlets.

FILLET OF PORK AU GRATIN

COOKING TIME: 40 mins. TEMPERATURE: E.375 – 400°F (190 – 200°C) G.5 – 6. QUANTITIES for 4

1 oz dried bread (25 g): 1 oz cheese (25 g)

Break the bread in small pieces and cut up the cheese. Drop the pieces through the top of the goblet with the motor running at slow speed. Blend to grate finely. Tip out and put aside.

8 oz sliced mushrooms (250 g): 1 oz butter (25 g)

Fry the mushrooms in the hot butter until they are just tender. Put the mushrooms and butter in the blender goblet

½ pt stock (250 ml) or use a mixture of double cream and wine: 2 Tbs tomato paste: 2 Tbs flour: Salt and pepper

Add to the mushrooms and blend smooth.

1 – 1½ lb fillet of pork (½ – ¾ kg): Lard

Cut the pork in ½ to 1 inch slices (1 cm) and fry it in hot lard until brown on both sides. Put it in a baking dish. Pour off any fat and add the mushroom mixture to the pan. Stir until it boils and pour it over the meat. Top with the crumbs and cheese and bake for about 20 minutes to finish cooking the meat and brown the crumbs.

PORK CHOPS WITH SWEET CORN

COOKING TIME: 1¾ hrs. TEMPERATURE: E.350°F (180°C) G.4. QUANTITIES for 4

4 pork chops: 1 Tbs oil

Trim surplus fat from the chops and brown them in the hot oil. Put them in a single layer in a casserole or baking dish.

2 Tbs evaporated milk

Pour off the fat from the frying pan, add the milk and mix to incorporate all the brown bits from the pan. Leave to stand.

2 oz bread (50 g): 6 oz canned sweet corn kernels or niblets (150 g)

Break the bread in pieces and blend it to fine crumbs. Tip into a bowl and add the corn. Mix.

1 egg: 2 Tbs evaporated milk: 1 small onion, cut up: 1 small green pepper cut up :1 tsp salt

Put in the goblet and blend to chop the vegetables. Add to the crumbs, and corn, with the heavy gravy from the frying pan. Mix well and spread on top of the chops. Cover the dish with a lid or with foil and bake for 1½ hours or until the meat is tender.

Serve hot with a green vegetable or cold with salad.

PORK IN SOUR SWEET SAUCE

COOKING TIME: about 45 mins. QUANTITIES for 4

1 lb lean boneless pork (500 g): 1 oz lard (25 g)

Cut the pork in slices about ½ inch thick (1 cm) and then in pieces about 1 inch square (2 cm.) Heat the lard and fry the meat quickly to brown it on both sides. Remove from the pan and pour off any fat remaining in the pan.

1 small onion cut in half: 2 tsp vinegar: 1 Tbs brown sugar: 1 Tbs lemon juice: 1 tsp tomato paste: 2 tsp Worcester or Soya sauce: 1 tsp mustard: ½ pt water or stock (150 ml): ½ tsp salt: ¼ tsp paprika: 2 tsp cornflour

Put all in the goblet and blend smooth. Add to the pan and stir until it boils. Return the meat to the sauce.

2 – 3 oz pineapple pieces (50 – 75 g) or mixed sweet pickles

Add to the meat, cover and simmer for 30 minutes, on top, or in the oven; until the meat is tender. Add more stock or water as needed during the cooking.

Alternative. Instead of the pineapple add 12 cooked and stoned prunes. To remove stones, steam the prunes for ½ hour, cool and stone.

VEAL AND HAM BLANQUETTE

This is not a classical blanquette because the colour of the bacon gives the dish a pinkish tinge. It is delicious, with a fine smooth sauce, and very easy to make.

COOKING TIME: 1½ hrs. QUANTITIES for 6

½ pt stock or water (250 ml): 1 medium onion: 2 oz mild fat bacon (50 g): 1 oz butter or margarine (25 g): 1 oz cornflour (25 g): 1 tsp salt: Pinch of pepper

Remove rinds and any bone from the bacon rashers and cut each in several pieces. Peel and quarter the onion. Put all ingredients in the goblet and blend until the onion is chopped finely. Tip into a pan and bring to the boil, stirring occasionally.

2 lb breast or pie veal cut in small pieces (1 kg)

Add the meat to the sauce and cook gently on top or in the oven until the meat is tender. If you cook it on top you may need to add more liquid to prevent it from sticking to the pan but don't make too much gravy.

1 egg yolk: 2 Tbs cream: 2 Tbs lemon juice

Put in the goblet with a little of the meat sauce. Blend smooth and pour into the rest of the meat and sauce. Stir to mix well and then serve.

Chapter Fifteen

VEGETABLES

The main use of the blender in vegetable preparation and cooking is either in chopping raw vegetables prior to cooking them or using them in salads, or in making vegetable purées for various types of recipes.

Cut the vegetables for chopping in pieces or leave them whole according to the type of blender. To chop small amounts feed them in through the top with the motor running at fast speed and chop as finely as required. For large amounts, cover the vegetables with cold water, blend for about 5 seconds or less. Drain on a sieve, reserving the liquid if stock is required.

Soft raw or cooked vegetables can be pulped without added liquid though it is usually easier if about ¼ pt (150 ml) of liquid is added for each pound (500 g) of vegetables.

With certain meats it is traditional to serve a vegetable purée, for example, turnip purée with mutton; carrot purée with lamb cutlets or veal; spinach purée with veal. Potato purée is not usually satisfactory when made in the blender as the result is generally too waxy in texture to suit most tastes.

Use the blender to make stuffings for baked or braised vegetables like stuffed green peppers, aubergines, onions, marrows and tomatoes.

The tougher vegetables can be blender-chopped for salads, for example, cabbage for Cole Slaw, carrots, turnips, green peppers and onions. They can either be chopped dry or in water and then drained.

ARTICHOKE MOULD
(a good dish for a light meal)

COOKING TIME: 1¼ hrs. QUANTITIES for 4

1 lb Jerusalem artichokes (500 g): ½ pt milk (250 ml)

Peel the artichokes and cut large ones in pieces. Boil in the milk for 15 – 20 minutes. Lift out and keep the milk for a sauce.

2 eggs: ¼ pt double cream (150 ml): Salt and pepper. Ground nutmeg or mace

Add these to the artichokes in the blender goblet. Process until smooth and pour into a well-oiled 1½ pint (¾ l) mould or basin. Cover with foil and steam for 1 hour.

Cheese, Parsley or other sauce, including the milk used in cooking the artichokes: Green peas

Turn the mould out onto a hot dish, mask with the sauce, and garnish with the peas.

COLD ASPARAGUS MOULD

This is suitable for a buffet or for a cold meal.

QUANTITIES for 4 – 6

12 – 15 oz can of asparagus (about 375 g): ½ oz gelatine (1½ Tbs)

If green asparagus is used the mould has a delicate green colour, the white spears give a creamy coloured mould. The green usually has the better flavour. Drain the asparagus. Heat the liquid to boiling, remove from the heat, leave a minute and then put in the goblet. Add the gelatine and blend on slow speed for a few seconds.

¼ pt evaporated milk (150 ml): Salt: Cayenne pepper

Put these in the goblet with the asparagus and blend for about 1 minute or until quite smooth. Pour into a 1 – 1½ pt (½ – 1 l) mould and leave to set. Cover and store in the refrigerator. Unmould onto a serving dish and garnish with

Chopped cooked ham or rolled slices of ham

STUFFED AUBERGINES

COOKING TIME: ½ hr. TEMPERATURE: E.375°F (190°C) G.5.
QUANTITIES for 4

Dry breadcrumbs: Grated cheese

If no dry bread is available, crumb a few dry biscuits by blending at slow speed. Likewise grate an ounce or so of cheese. Set aside to use later.

4 aubergines: Oil

Wash and cut in half lengthwise. With the point of a sharp knife criss-cross the flesh to within an inch of the skin (2 cm). Fry them, cut side down, in a little hot oil for about 7 minutes. Cool. Remove the pulp leaving enough round the edges to retain the original shape of the aubergine. Put the pulp in the blender.

8 oz sliced mushrooms (250 g): ½ oz cheese (a small cube): 1 egg: Salt and pepper

Put in the goblet and mix to chop the mushrooms and grate the cheese. Tip the mixture into a bowl. If it seems too wet, add some of the dry breadcrumbs but avoid making it stodgy. Put the aubergine shells in a baking dish and fill them with the mixture. Sprinkle the tops liberally with dried crumbs and grated cheese and bake for about 20 minutes or until the tops are lightly browned.

BROAD BEAN PURÉE
(to serve with ham or boiled bacon)

QUANTITIES: for 4

2 x 10½ oz cans broad beans (595 g): 2 sprigs parsley

Empty the beans and the liquid in the cans into the goblet. Blend to a smooth purée, adding parsley towards the end and just blending enough to chop it.

1 oz butter (25 g): Mashed potato powder

Melt the butter in a pan and add the purée. Bring to the boil. Add enough potato powder to make the mixture the desired consistency. Adjust seasoning and serve.

GREEN BEAN AND APPLE SALAD

QUANTITIES for 4

8 oz cooked whole French beans, fresh or frozen; or use sliced green beans (250 g)

Cut the whole beans in pieces and put them in a basin.

1 small dessert apple: 1 stick of celery

Peel, core and cut the apples in pieces. Cut up the celery. Blend these separately or together, just to chop them. Use the on/off technique. Add to the beans.

Salt and pepper: Mayonnaise or other dressing

Add enough dressing to moisten, and season if necessary.

COLE SLAW

QUANTITIES for 4

4 oz shelled walnuts (125 g): 8 oz white cabbage (250 g)

Blend the nuts on/off to chop them coarsely. Tip out of the goblet. Wash the cabbage and cut it in rough pieces. Put it in the goblet and cover with cold water. Blend on/off just to chop. Strain and press out surplus moisture.

4 Tbs mayonnaise: Salt and pepper

Mix cabbage and nuts with the mayonnaise and season to taste. Serve at once or store in the refrigerator.

Alternative. In place of the nuts use a slice of onion blended with the cabbage; or a slice of green pepper; or a small dessert apple.

DOLMAS
(Stuffed Cabbage Leaves)

COOKING TIME: 30 mins. QUANTITIES for 4

4 large cabbage leaves or 8 small ones

Pour boiling water over the leaves and let them stand for a minute or two to make them pliable. Drain.

8 oz cold cooked meat (250 g)

Remove skin and gristle and cut the meat in pieces. Blend to shred it finely and tip into a basin.

1 slice of onion: 2 sprigs of parsley: Some fresh or dried thyme and marjoram: 1 egg: Salt and pepper

Put all in the goblet and blend until the onion and herbs are chopped. Add to the meat and combine well. Put a little filling on each cabbage leaf and roll up like a parcel, starting with the stem end.

4 rashers streaky bacon: White wine

Remove rinds and put the rashers flat in the bottom of a sauce-pan. Add the cabbage leaves, touching one another, and moisten with a little wine or water. Cover the pan and simmer for 30 minutes. Serve with the liquid and the bacon. Boiled rice makes a good accompaniment.

Alternative. Lift the cabbage and bacon from the pan and keep hot. Thicken the liquid with an egg yolk and 2 Tbs lemon juice, in the blender.

CARROT MOULD WITH GREEN PEAS

This makes a very decorative vegetable for a special meal. The orange-coloured mould contrasts well with the green peas.

COOKING TIME: $\frac{1}{2}$ – $\frac{3}{4}$ hr. TEMPERATURE: E.350°F (180°C) G.4.
QUANTITIES for 4

$\frac{1}{4}$ *pt single cream or evaporated milk (150 ml): 8 oz cooked or canned carrots, drained (250 g): Salt and pepper: 1 slice of onion: 1 egg*

Put all ingredients in the goblet and blend until smooth. Pour into a well-oiled ring mould, $\frac{3}{4}$ pint size (400 ml). Stand this in a baking tin of hot water and cook until firm. Remove from the water and leave the mould to stand for a few minutes before turning out on a hot dish.

8 oz fresh or frozen green peas (250 g): Knob of butter

Boil the peas, drain, and toss in the butter to coat them. Pile them in the centre of the ring mould and serve hot.

CARROT PURÉE
(to serve with grilled lamb cutlets or with veal)

QUANTITIES for 4

1$\frac{1}{2}$ lb cooked or canned carrots (750 g): 1 small onion, cut up: $\frac{1}{2}$ oz dripping (1 Tbs): Salt and pepper

Drain the carrots. Blend the onion to chop it. Melt the fat and fry the onion until it just begins to brown. Blend the carrots to a purée. Add to the onions, mix, heat and season to taste.

Should it be too sloppy, heat a little to drive off some of the water, or add a little mashed potato powder to thicken it.

CAULIFLOWER WITH WALNUTS

COOKING TIME: 20 – 30 mins. QUANTITIES for 4

1 oz bread (25 g): 1 oz shelled walnuts (25 g)

Cut the crusts from the bread and spread it with butter or margarine. Cut in small pieces and put in the goblet with the walnuts. Blend on/off at slow speed until the bread is in crumbs and the nuts chopped. Tip into a small bowl.

½ pt hot milk (250 ml): 1 oz flour (25 g): 1 oz margarine (25 g): Salt and pepper

Put in the goblet and blend for a few seconds to mix well. Pour into the pan and heat and stir until it boils. Boil for 2 – 3 minutes and keep hot, stirring occasionally.

1 medium cauliflower, in sprigs

Boil in a little salted water until just tender. Drain and arrange in a baking dish. Mask with the sauce and sprinkle the crumb mixture over the top. Brown under the grill or in a hot oven.

PURÉE OF CELERY
(to serve with poultry, pork or lamb)

COOKING TIME: 20 – 30 mins. QUANTITIES for 4

1 lb celery, including the small tender leaves (500 g): ¼ pt water (150 ml) and 1 chicken cube or use ¼ pt chicken stock

Wash the celery and slice it fairly coarsely. Boil the water and dissolve the chicken cube in it, or boil the stock. Add the celery and boil until it is just tender. Put in the goblet with the liquid.

¼ pt milk (150 ml): ½ oz butter (1 Tbs)

Add to the celery and blend to a fine purée. Tip back into the pan and bring to the boil.

Mashed potato powder

Draw the pan off the heat and add potato powder to make the mixture the desired consistency, not too stodgy.

Salt and pepper: Ground mace or nutmeg

Season to taste and serve hot.

STUFFED CUCUMBER

COOKING TIME: 30 – 45 mins. TEMPERATURE: E.375°F (190°C) G.5.

QUANTITIES for 4

1 medium sized cucumber

Peel and cut in half lengthwise, removing the seeds to make a cavity for the stuffing. Alternatively, cut the cucumber across into 8 pieces and remove enough of the centres to make a cup for stuffing.

1 oz bread (25 g): 1 oz cheese (25 g)

Break the bread in pieces and cut up the cheese. Blend together on slow speed to crumb the bread and grate the cheese. Tip into a basin.

2 oz cooked ham or other meat (50 g)

Cut in pieces and blend at slow speed to shred it. Add to the crumbs.

White stock: Salt and pepper: Garlic salt

Add to the meat mixture using enough stock to bind. Put the prepared cucumber in a baking dish and fill the centres with the mixture. Pour a little stock in the bottom of the dish and bake until the cucumber is tender. Just before serving, pour over a little of

Tomato or other sauce.

LEEK PUREÉ

Serve this with roast or fried meat such as veal or chicken, or use it as a dish for a light meal, served with grilled bacon, or gammon.

COOKING TIME: 20 mins. QUANTITIES for 4

2 lb trimmed leeks (1 kg)

Split in half and wash very thoroughly. Boil in a little salted water until tender, drain and allow to cool a little.

1 egg: ¼ pt cream or evaporated milk (150 ml): Grated nutmeg: Pepper

Put these in the goblet with the leeks and blend smooth.
   ½ oz butter (1 Tbs)

Melt in a pan and add the purée. Heat gently until it thickens. Taste for seasoning and serve hot.

NUT LOAF

For a vegetarian meal serve this hot with a savoury sauce as a main dish, or cold, with salad. It also makes a good accompaniment to meat such as pork, ham or veal, in place of an ordinary vegetable.

COOKING TIME: 1 hr. TEMPERATURE: E.375°F (190°C) G.5.
QUANTITIES for a 1 lb loaf (500 g)

1 oz cornflakes (25 g)

Blend these to make fine crumbs. Grease the loaf tin heavily and dust it with the crumbs.

4 oz wholemeal bread (125 g): 4 oz nuts (125 g)

Break up the bread and blend it in two lots to make crumbs. Tip into a mixing bowl. Blend the nuts to chop them, and add to the crumbs.

1 egg: ¼ pt milk (150 ml): 1 oz soft butter or margarine (25 g): Salt and pepper: 2 slices of onion: 1 medium carrot, cut up: Fresh herbs

Put all in the goblet and blend to chop the vegetables. Add to the crumbs and nuts and mix thoroughly. Put in the prepared tin and smooth the top. Bake until lightly browned and firm. Turn out on a serving dish.

ORANGE SALAD
(to serve with chicken, pork or veal)

QUANTITIES for 4

4 medium oranges

Peel them and slice very thinly over a plate to catch the juice. Remove the pips and put the fruit in a shallow dish, reserving the juice.

1 small onion: 4 Tbs olive oil: ½ tsp salt

Put the orange juice in the goblet with the peeled and cut up onion, oil and salt. Blend until the onion is finely chopped. Pour the mixture over the oranges and leave to marinate for 20 minutes.

Lettuce leaves

Arrange the orange slices in a bed of lettuce leaves.

PARSNIP BALLS
(to serve with fish)

COOKING TIME: 40 mins. TEMPERATURE: E4.400°F (200°C) G.6. QUANTITIES for 4

1 lb parsnips (500 g): Mashed potato powder: Salt and pepper

Peel, cut and boil the parsnips until tender. Drain. Put them in the blender to make a purée. Tip into a basin and add enough mashed potato powder to make a dough firm enough to roll into balls. Season well.

Dried bread or crusts, or dry biscuits

Break into pieces and drop through the top of the goblet with the motor running at low speed. Blend to make fine crumbs. Shape the parsnip mixture into small balls and roll them in the crumbs to coat them well. Bake them with baked fish or by themselves for about 20 minutes or until lightly browned.

Alternative. Blend a few walnuts to chop them and add to the parsnip and potato mixture.

PARNSIP AND CARROT PURÉE

COOKING TIME: 20 mins. QUANTITIES for 6 – 8

1 lb parsnips (500 g): 1 lb carrots (500 g)

Peel the parsnips and scrape the carrots. Cut both in pieces and boil separately in a little salted water until tender. Blend to a purée separately using the minimum amount of cooking water needed for easy blending. Mix the two purées and return to the pan to heat and dry a little.

Knob of butter: Salt and pepper

Add the butter and taste for seasoning. Serve hot. Should it by any chance become too sloppy, add a little mashed potato powder to correct the consistency.

GREEN PEA PURÉE WITH EGGS AND BACON

This is a very good dish for a light meal.

COOKING TIME: 15 – 20 mins. QUANTITIES for 4

1 lb frozen peas or shelled new peas (500 g)

Boil the peas until tender in a little salted water. Drain, reserving the stock. Blend the peas to a purée, using as much of the cooking liquid as necessary to moisten. Re-heat in the pan.

4 Tbs cream: 1 oz butter (25 g): Potato powder

Add cream and butter to the purée and enough mashed potato powder to make it a fairly stiff consistency. Put the mixture in four mounds on hot plates and put to keep hot.

8 oz bacon (250 g): 4 eggs

Remove the rinds and cut the bacon in small pieces. Fry until it is crisp. Poach the eggs. Put an egg on each portion of the purée and sprinkle the bacon round it.

SPINACH AU BEURRE

QUANTITIES for 4 – 6

2 lb spinach (1 kg), fresh or frozen

Wash the spinach and cook it without any added water. When it is tender, drain it well.

Salt and pepper: Pinch grated nutmeg or mace: Squeeze of lemon juice.

Put these in the blender with the spinach and mix to a purée.

2 oz butter (50 g)

Melt the butter in the pan, add the purée and re-heat. If the spinach seems watery, increase the heat to evaporate the moisture.

SPINACH AU GRATIN WITH MUSHROOMS

A good dish for the main course of a light meal.

COOKING TIME: 30 – 40 mins. TEMPERATURE: E.400°F (200°C) G.6.

QUANTITIES for 4 – 6

7 oz firm strong cheese (200 g)

Cut the cheese in pieces and blend at slow speed in two or more lots to grate it. Tip into a bowl.

2 onions, cut up: 1 Tbs oil: 4 oz sliced mushrooms (125 g): Salt and pepper

Blend the onions dry, to chop them. Heat the oil and stew the onions gently until they are tender and beginning to soften. Add the mushrooms and seasoning and stew until the onions are tender. Keep warm.

2 lb spinach (1 kg): 1 oz butter (25 g): 1 Tbs oil

Wash the spinach and put it in a pan with the oil. Cover and cook until just tender, drain and chop roughly. Grease a baking dish and put the spinach, onion mixture, and cheese in it in layers, finishing with a topping of cheese. Dot the cheese with butter and bake near the top of the oven for about 20 minutes, to brown the cheese.

TOMATOES AU GRATIN

COOKING TIME: 20 mins. TEMPERATURE: E.375°F (190°C) G.5.

QUANTITIES for 4

1 oz bread (25 g)

Break the bread in pieces and blend to make fine crumbs. Tip out.

1 small onion: 2 sprigs parsley

Skin onion and cut in half. Blend with the parsley until finely chopped. Put an ounce of melted fat or 2 tablespoons of oil in a shallow baking dish. Sprinkle in the onion mixture.

4 large tomatoes: 2 Tbs oil: Salt and Pepper

Cut the tomatoes in half and put in the dish, sprinkle with salt and pepper, using a little garlic salt if liked. Sprinkle the breadcrumbs on top of the tomatoes and then sprinkle on the oil. Bake near the top of the oven until the tomatoes are tender and lightly browned on top.

STUFFED TOMATOES

COOKING TIME: 20 mins. TEMPERATURE: E.375°F (190°C) G.5.
QUANTITIES for 4 – 8

8 medium tomatoes, firm ripe

Wash and cut a slice off the stem end. With a small spoon scoop out the pulp taking care not to break the skin. Season the insides with salt and pepper, including a little garlic salt if liked. Put the tomatoes in a shallow greased baking dish.

2 oz bread (50 g)

Tear in pieces and blend to make crumbs. Tip into a bowl.

½ oz cheese (a small cube): 2 anchovy fillets: 2 oz cooked ham (50 g): 1 sprig parsley: Pepper

Cut the ham in strips and put these ingredients in the goblet with the tomato pulp. Blend until smooth and add to the breadcrumbs. Mix well and use to fill the tomatoes. Put slice on top. Bake until the tomatoes are cooked but not broken.

TURNIP PURÉE
(to serve with lamb or mutton)

COOKING TIME: 20 – 30 mins. QUANTITIES for 4

1 lb turnips (500 g): Salt

Peel the turnips, cut them in pieces and boil in a little salted water until they are tender. Drain and blend to a purée, using some of the cooking liquid as needed to moisten.

1 oz butter (25 g): Freshly ground pepper: Mashed potato powder

Return the purée to the pan and re-heat it with the butter. Add potato powder to give it the desired consistency. Add pepper to taste and serve hot.

Chapter Sixteen

COLD SWEETS

Cold sweets or puddings made with a fruit purée can be made much faster using the blender and you get more flavour because less fruit is wasted than when sieving to make a purée.

To purée firm fruit add either water, fruit juice, evaporated milk or other liquid to 1 lb (500 g) of the fruit. Cut the fruit in pieces, removing stones and cores. Blend on slow speed until the purée begins to rise and then switch to fast speed. With cooked or raw juicy fruits no liquid is needed. Purées made with fruit containing very small seeds may need to be strained before use.

Ingredients frequently used in recipes for cold sweets and which are not suitable for blending but need to be beaten separately, are egg whites and whipped cream; though when the cream is not important as a bulking agent to add air to the mixture, it may be blended with the other ingredients.

Extra fast setting for sweets made with gelatine can be achieved by substituting some crushed ice for some of the liquid in the recipe, blending in the ice after the gelatine has been dissolved. When calculating how much ice can be added, count $\frac{1}{2}$ pint coarsely crushed ice (250 ml) as equal to $\frac{1}{4}$ pint (150 ml) of water.

For mousses and cold soufflés where the normal method is to make a gelatine mixture and cool this until it almost sets, before adding whipped cream and egg whites, the cooling process may be speeded up by blending in some crushed ice and adding the cream with the motor running at full speed. This usually makes the mixture cold and thick enough to add the beaten egg whites straight away. The final dish will then set very quickly.

APPLE FOOL

QUANTITIES for 4

> *1 lb apples (500 g): 2 Tbs lemon juice: 8 Tbs evaporated milk: 3 oz sugar (75 g): Pinch of cinnamon*

Peel, core and cut the apples in small pieces. Blend the ingredients together in one or more lots, using the on/off technique. Blend until smooth. Pour into individual glasses and serve at once.

Crisp biscuits (like hazel nut biscuits): Cream

Serve these as optional accompaniments.

APRICOT MOULD

QUANTITIES for 4 – 6

1 x 29 oz can apricot halves (820 g): ½ oz gelatine (1½ Tbs) dissolved in 3 Tbs hot water: Kirsch or almond essence

Blend the contents of the can with the dissolved gelatine, in one or more lots depending on the machine. Flavour to taste and pour into 1½ pint mould (1 l). Refrigerate until set. Unmould and serve with cream. Garnish with fruit.

APRICOT PURÉE WITH ALMONDS

QUANTITIES for 4 – 6

8 oz dried apricots (250 g)

Wash the apricots and put them in a pan with water to cover well. Simmer, without a lid, for 30 minutes.

4 oz sugar (125 g)

Add to the apricots and simmer for 5 minutes. Cool, and blend in one or more lots according to the capacity of the blender, remembering that the thicker the mixture the less the blender can manage at a time. Only add water if the mixture seems too thick to blend.

2 Tbs blanched almonds

Add these to the last blending or add a few at a time and blend just enough to chop them coarsely. Chill the mixture in the refrigerator and serve with

Sweetened whipped cream

113

APRICOT FOOL

QUANTITIES for 4 – 6

Make the same mixture as above but omit the almonds. Allow the fruit to become quite cold before blending.

½ pt whipping cream (250 ml)

When the apricots are pulped open the top of the goblet and run the cream in slowly, mixing until light. Serve chilled, decorated with split almonds.

BANANA MOULD WITH STRAWBERRY SAUCE

QUANTITIES for 4

1 Tbs gelatine: 4 Tbs hot water

Dissolve the gelatine in the water.

8 oz ripe bananas (250 g): 1 oz sugar (25 g) or to taste: ½ pt single cream (250 ml): 1 Tbs lemon juice

Skin the bananas and cut them up roughly. Put in the blender goblet with the cream, sugar, lemon and dissolved gelatine. Blend until smooth and light. Pour into individual moulds or into a 1 pt (½ l) mould. Leave to set.

8 oz fresh or partially thawed frozen strawberries (250 g): Sugar to taste

Blend the fruit and sugar to make a sauce. Unmould the banana mixture and pour the sauce over it.

BANANA MOUSSE

QUANTITIES for 4 – 6

1 lb bananas (500 g): 1 Tbs lemon juice: 2 Tbs sugar: ¼ pt yogurt (150 ml): 4 Tbs double cream

Skin the bananas and cut up roughly. Put them in the goblet with the other ingredients. Blend until smooth.

2 egg whites

Beat until stiff enough to stand up in peaks. Add the banana mixture and combine thoroughly. Cover and put in the refrigerator to chill. It thickens a little and turns a pale beige colour. Serve garnished with

Chopped toasted almonds or grated chocolate.

BANANA WHIP

QUANTITIES for 4

4 bananas: 8 Tbs cream or evaporated milk: 2 Tbs lemon juice: 4 Tbs sugar (or less to taste)

Skin the bananas and cut in pieces. Put in the goblet with the other ingredients and blend until smooth. This will be a fairly sloppy mixture but it thickens when stored in the refrigerator in a covered dish for an hour or so.

Glacé cherries, chopped walnuts or grated chocolate

Serve in individual dishes, decorated to taste.

CHESTNUT FOOL

QUANTITIES for 4 – 6

1 lb fresh or canned chestnut purée (500 g): 2 Tbs rum: 2 oz icing sugar (50g): 1 tsp vanilla: ¼ pt evaporated milk (150 ml)

Blend the ingredients in two or more lots, depending on the capacity of the blender. Put some of the evaporated milk in the bottom of the blender first. Blend until smooth and light, about 1 minute. Pour into individual dishes and chill in the refrigerator.

Grated chocolate or cold chocolate sauce.

Cover the top with a layer of chocolate and serve.

CHOCOLATE MOUSSE

These are the ingredients of a classical chocolate mousse but the method is adapted to the blender. It is much simpler than the old method and more reliable.

QUANTITIES for 4

3 egg whites

115

Whip until the mixture stands up in peaks. Leave to stand while the other ingredients are blended.

3 oz bitter or semi-sweet chocolate (75 g): 3 egg yolks: 3 Tbs hot water: 1 Tbs rum or brandy

Break the chocolate into small pieces and put all the ingredients in the goblet. Blend on slow speed until the chocolate is melted and the mixture smooth. Tip out into the egg whites and combine thoroughly. Pour into individual serving dishes, cover and refrigerate for several hours or overnight.

CHOCOLATE AND ORANGE MOULD

QUANTITIES for 4 – 6

1 orange jelly (enough to make 1 pt or ½ l): ¼ pt hot water (150 ml)

Put the water in the goblet and add the broken up jelly. Blend on slow speed to dissolve the jelly.

3 – 4 oz bitter or semi-sweet chocolate (75 – 125 g)

Break in pieces and add to the goblet, blending on slow speed to melt it.

½ pt crushed ice (250 ml)

Add to the goblet and blend for a few seconds. At this stage it may be necessary to remove some of the mixture to make room for the cream.

¼ pt double cream or evaporated milk (150 ml)

Set the motor running at high speed, remove the top and slowly pour in the cream or milk. Blend for 30 seconds. If this has been done in two lots, combine the mixtures and pour into an oiled mould. Cover and put in the refrigerator to set.

Sliced fresh oranges or canned tangerine oranges

Unmould and garnish with the oranges. Fresh ones are nicer because the mould is already well sweetened.

COFFEE BAVAROIS

These are the classical ingredients of a Bavarois but the method has been adapted for the blender. Other Bavarois can be made in a similar way.

1 Tbs gelatine: ¼ pt hot milk (150 ml): 2 oz sugar (50 g)

Put gelatine and sugar in the goblet and add the hot milk. Blend on slow speed to dissolve the gelatine.

2 egg yolks: 1 Tbs soluble coffee

Add and blend for a few seconds.

¼ pt crushed ice (150 ml): ¼ pt double cream (150 ml)

With the motor running at full speed, remove the goblet cover and add the ice, and then the cream in a steady stream. Blend for 30 seconds longer. Pour into individual serving dishes or into a mould to set. Garnish with

Whipped cream and chopped nuts.

COFFEE CHEESE CREAM

This is a rich, concentrated sweet and a small portion is usually sufficient, especially if it comes at the end of a substantial meal. In that case, serve it in small wine glasses, making 4 – 5 portions.

QUANTITIES for 3 or more

¼ pt double cream (150 ml): 2 Tbs caster sugar: 1 Tbs brandy: 2 tsp instant coffee: 8 oz cottage cheese (250 g)

Put all ingredients in the goblet, in two lots if necessary, and blend until quite smooth. Put in individual serving dishes and refrigerate for several hours to chill well.

FRUIT ICE CREAM

QUANTITIES for 4

About 8 oz fruit (250 g)

The fruit can be raw or frozen, berries being the best; but bananas, drained canned pineapples, or cooked dried apricots are also suitable. If the fruit is frozen, partially thaw it before blending it to a pulp. Stewed or canned fruit should be drained before using or the resulting pulp will be too thin; the less watery the better.

117

1 oz icing sugar (25 g): ¼ pt whipping cream (150 ml)

Add the icing sugar to the fruit pulp, using more or less according to taste. Blend to dissolve the sugar. Whip the cream but stop before it gets really stiff. Fold the fruit mixture into it. Freeze without stirring.

Be very careful not to over-whip the cream or the finished ice cream will have an unpleasant grainy, greasy texture.

When using frozen fruit which is only partially thawed it is possible to pour the cream into the blended purée, using high speed. Avoid blending too long or a buttery texture will result.

HAZEL NUT ICE CREAM

QUANTITIES for 6

2 oz toasted and skinned hazel nuts (50 g): 1 oz caster sugar (25 g): ¼ pt evaporated milk (150 ml)

Put the nuts in the goblet and blend until finely ground. Add the sugar and milk and blend again, scraping down as necessary.

¼ pt whipping cream (150 ml)

Whip the cream until light but not stiff. Add the blended mixture to it and combine thoroughly. Pour into the freezing tray and freeze without stirring.

To Toast Hazel Nuts. Put them in a baking tin in a moderate oven until they begin to brown and the skins will rub off easily. Cool, rub off the skins and pick out the nuts. Do this in a colander and most of the skins will fall away.

MARMALADE DE PRUNEAUX

COOKING TIME: ½ – ¾ hr. QUANTITIES for 4

8 oz prunes (250 g)

Soak the prunes overnight in cold water to cover well. Next day boil until soft. Strain, cool a little and remove the stones. Put the prunes in the blender goblet.

½ oz sugar (1 Tbs)

Add to the prune juice and boil rapidly until the juice is reduced by about half.

3 oz red wine or port (90 ml)

Add to the prunes and blend to a smooth purée. Add to the prune syrup and cook until the mixture is the consistency of a thick sauce or purée. Cool and then store in the refrigerator. Serve in individual dishes with or without

Cream.

MOCHA ICE CREAM

QUANTITIES for 8

½ pt hot water (250 ml): 4 oz plain chocolate (125 g)

Put the water in the warmed goblet and add the chocolate broken in pieces. Blend on low speed to melt the chocolate.

¼ pt evaporated milk (150 g): 1 Tbs rum or ½ tsp vanilla: 1 Tbs soluble coffee

Add to the chocolate mixture and blend for 30 seconds. Tip into a bowl and leave to become quite cold.

¼ pt whipping cream (150 ml)

Whip the cream lightly but not until it is stiff. Whisk it into the chocolate mixture and pour into freezing trays. When the mixture is beginning to freeze round the edges stir to mix well.

Alternative. If bitter or semi-sweet chocolate is preferred, blend 1 – 2 oz icing sugar (25 – 50 g) when adding the milk.

PAIN DE FRUIT

COOKING TIME: 15 – 20 mins. QUANTITIES for 4

¼ pt lemon or lime jelly (150 ml)

Use a packet jelly for this and put it in the bottom of a 1 – 1½ pt mould (1 l). Put to set.

1 lb apples (500 g): ½ pt water (250 ml): 4 oz sugar (125 g) or to taste: 1 strip lemon rind

Peel, core and slice the apples and stew them slowly with the other ingredients until the fruit is soft.

½ oz gelatine (1½ Tbs) soaked in 2 Tbs cold water

Put the soft fruit and lemon rind in the blender goblet with the soaked gelatine and blend until smooth, about 1 minute. Cool until it is just beginning to set and then pour it carefully on top of the lemon jelly. When set unmould, garnish with fruit and serve with cream.

Alternative. Set a garnish of fruit, glacé, fresh or canned, in the lemon or lime jelly, before adding the apple mixture.

PEACHES CARDINAL

QUANTITIES for 4

8 canned or fresh peach halves: 8 oz fresh or frozen raspberries (250 g): Caster sugar: Kirsch

Fresh peaches should be dipped in boiling water for a minute and then in cold before skinning. Don't do this until the raspberry mixture is ready as the peaches discolour if exposed to the air. Canned peaches should be drained thoroughly. Put the fruit in a shallow serving dish or in individual dishes.

Frozen raspberries should be partially thawed. Blend fresh or frozen, with sugar to taste, to make a smooth purée. Strain to remove seeds, add kirsch to taste and pour over the peaches.

Silvered almonds

Garnish with almonds.

PINEAPPLE AND WALNUT MOUSSE

This is an old recipe for a light sweet in which the walnuts used to be pounded to a powder in a mortar. I have adapted it to the blender method.

QUANTITIES for 4 – 6

16 oz can of small pineapple chunks or pieces (500 g)

Drain the pineapple, reserving the juice. Heat $\frac{1}{4}$ pt (150 ml) of the juice to just under boiling.

$\frac{1}{4}$ – $\frac{3}{4}$ oz gelatine (1$\frac{1}{2}$ – 2 Tbs)

If a soft mousse is preferred, use the smaller amount of gelatine. Put it in the goblet with the hot juice and blend on slow speed for a second or two. Add the pineapple chunks and remaining juice.

2 egg yolks: 2 oz shelled walnuts (50 g): A scant ½ pt crushed ice (250 ml)

Add the egg yolks and nuts and blend to chop nuts and pineapple finely. With the motor running at fast speed, open the top of the goblet and add the ice. Blend for 30 seconds.

2 egg whites

Beat until stiff, add the blended mixture and combine gently and thoroughly. Pour into a soufflé dish or other serving dish and, when it is quite cold, refrigerate until required. Garnish to taste with

Whipped cream: Walnuts: Pineapple.

PRALINE ICE CREAM

QUANTITIES for 6

4 oz praline (125 g)

For making praline, see page 143.

3 oz sugar (75 g): 3 Tbs water

Combine in a small pan, stir until boiling and boil hard for 3 minutes.

2 eggs or 4 yolks: 1 tsp vanilla

Put in the goblet and blend for a few seconds. Then remove the top of the goblet while the motor is running at full speed, pour the hot syrup into the eggs in a steady stream, taking care not to let it fall on the sides of the goblet or it will set as toffee. Blend for about 30 seconds. Turn into a basin, stand this in cold water, and whisk until the mixture is cold, or whisk occasionally as it cools.

½ pt whipping cream (250 ml)

Soft whip the cream and fold it into the egg mixture. Avoid over-whipping or the ice cream will have a grainy texture. Freeze until almost set, then stir well and mix in the praline. Continue freezing.

PRUNE AND PINEAPPLE FOOL

QUANTITIES for 4

¼ pt milk (150 ml): 1 Tbs custard powder

Blend to mix. Pour into a small pan and stir until boiling, simmer a minute or so. Set aside to cool.

12 oz cooked or canned prunes (375 g): 4 oz drained canned pineapple pieces (125 g): Caster sugar

Stone the prunes and put them in the goblet. Add the pineapple and blend to a smooth purée. Taste for sweetness, adding sugar if required.

¼ pt double cream (150 ml)

Add with the cold custard and continue to blend until the mixture is thick and light. Put in individual dishes and store in the refrigerator until required.

Alternative. Add spices or liqueur for extra flavour.

YOGURT JELLY WHIP

QUANTITIES for 4

1 pt packet of lemon jelly (½ l)

Break up the jelly and put it in the blender goblet with ½ pt hot water (250 ml). Blend on slow speed until the jelly is dissolved. Tip into a basin, cool and leave until it is beginning to set. Don't worry if it sets completely, but break it up again in the blender before adding the yogurt.

¼ pt yogurt (150 ml)

Add to the jelly and blend until light and frothy. Pour into a mould to set. Unmould and serve plain or with

Fruit or cream

Chapter Seventeen

SWEET FLANS AND TARTS

Short pastry, using half fat to flour, can be made in the blender. Use a firm fat, cut it in pieces and drop it into the flour in the goblet. Blend for just a second or so to mix. Unless you are very clever with the timing, the mixture may look a bit lumpy when you tip it out into the mixing bowl but, when water is added in the usual way, it mixes smoothly and makes an excellent short pastry.

In some blenders 4 oz flour (125 g) is the most you can mix successfully at a time, but the large broad-based goblets will take 8 oz (250 g) easily.

The popular uncooked or refrigerated flans are ideal for making in the blender using biscuit or cereal crumbs and are very quickly made

APRICOTS À LA BOURDALOUE

COOKING TIME: 40 mins. QUANTITIES for an 8 in. (20 cm) flan

4 oz self-raising flour (125 g): Pinch of salt: 1½ oz butter or margarine (40 g): 1 oz caster sugar (25 g): 1 egg yolk or ½ whole egg

Make these into a sweet pastry using the egg for mixing. Roll out to line the flan, prick the bottom and bake blind at 400°F (200°C) G.6 for 15 – 20 minutes. Remove from the flan ring and put on a serving dish.

2 oz macaroons (50 g)

Break in pieces and blend to fine crumbs. Tip into a basin.

4 oz caster sugar (125 g): 1 oz flour (25 g): 2 eggs: ½ pt hot milk (250 ml): Pinch of salt

Put in the goblet and blend smooth. Pour into the pan and stir and heat until it thickens. Cook for 2 – 3 minutes.

1½ oz butter (40 g)

Add to the sauce and stir until it melts. Add half the macaroon crumbs. Cool the mixture, stirring occasionally to prevent a skin from forming, or just leave to cool and then blend the skin in before using the sauce. This is the recipe for Frangipan Cream.

Not less than 1 lb of canned apricot halves or 1 lb fresh apricots poached in syrup (500 g)

Drain the fruit. Spread half the frangipan mixture on the bottom of the flan case. Arrange a layer of fruit on this, keeping back a few pieces for decoration. Cover the fruit with the rest of the mixture. Sprinkle the remaining macaroon crumbs over the top and garnish with fruit.

Alternative. Make the flan with other fruit such as bananas poached in vanilla-flavoured syrup; canned or fresh poached peaches; or use pears or apples.

BISCUIT FLAN

QUANTITIES for an 8 in. (20 cm) flan.

6 oz digestive biscuits (150 g): 1 Tbs honey or syrup: 3 oz butter (75 g) or half butter and half margarine: ¼ tsp cinnamon

Break up the biscuits and blend them in two or more lots, tipping each into a mixing bowl. Blend to fine crumbs. This is done either by putting the biscuits in with the motor off and then switching to slow speed; or by switching on to slow and dropping the pieces of biscuit through the top of the goblet, keeping one hand over the top to prevent the biscuits from flying out. Just melt the fat, honey and cinnamon and add to the crumbs. Stir to combine well. Put the flan ring on a serving dish, tip the mixture into the middle and use the back of a spoon to mould it to fit the flan. Mould the sides first and then spread the rest over the bottom. Chill to set the flan and remove the ring before adding the filling.

An alternative to the flan ring is to use a glass pie plate or a sandwich tin lined with foil. Peel off the foil when the flan has been refrigerated to make it firm.

Alternative. Use ginger biscuits in place of the digestive biscuits, specially good with a lemon filling.

CARROT FLAN

This is similar in texture to a pumpkin pie and has a pleasant spicy flavour.

COOKING TIME: 40 – 45 mins. TEMPERATURE: E.400°F (200°C) G.6.

QUANTITIES for a 6 – 7 in. (15 – 18 cm) flan.

Line the flan with short crust pastry and prick the base with a fork. Put in the refrigerator while the filling is being made.

1 egg: ¼ tsp cinnamon: 4 Tbs evaporated milk or single cream: ¼ tsp ground nutmeg or mace: Pinch of salt: Pinch of ground ginger: 2 oz light brown sugar (50 g): 8 oz cooked or canned carrots (250 g): Pinch of ground cloves.

Cut the carrots in pieces and put all ingredients in the goblet. Blend until smooth and then pour into the pastry case. Bake until the pastry is lightly browned and the filling is set. Serve warm or cold.

CHEESE CAKE PIE

COOKING TIME: 1 hr. TEMPERATURE: E.300°F (150°C) G.2.

QUANTITIES for an 8 – 9 in. flan or sandwich tin (20 – 25 cm).

Unless the 8 in. tin is a fairly deep one it is well to line it with foil and bring the foil a little above the top of the tin.

6 oz digestive biscuits (150 g)

Break these in pieces and blend them in several lots to give fine crumbs. Tip into a mixing bowl.

3 oz butter or margarine (75 g): 3 Tbs caster sugar: 1 Tbs golden syrup

Melt together but do not make hot. Add to the crumbs, mix well and press into the flan ring or sandwich tin, lined with foil. Put in the refrigerator to harden.

1 lb cottage cheese (500 g): 2 oz caster sugar (50 g): 2 eggs: 1 tsp vanilla essence: ¼ pt evaporated milk (150 ml)

Blend all together in two or more lots, until smooth, about 1 minute. Pour into the biscuit case. Bake until set. Allow to cool.

Cherry, strawberry or peach jam.

Remove the pie from its foil or flan and put on a serving dish. Spread the top with jam, if necessary, thinning the jam first by blending it with a little cold water. Serve the pie chilled.

CHOCOLATE FLAN

QUANTITIES for an 8 in. (20 cm) flan

8 oz chocolate digestive biscuits (250 g)

Break the biscuits in pieces and blend them in several lots on slow speed to make crumbs. Tip into a mixing bowl.

2 oz butter or margarine (50 g): 1 Tbs golden syrup

Heat just to melt but not make hot. Add to the crumbs and mix well. Press into the flan ring standing on a serving plate. Press up round the sides first and then spread the remaining mixture evenly over the bottom of the flan. Put in the refrigerator to set. Fill with fruit or a cooked filling.

HAZEL NUT TARTLETS

COOKING TIME: 15 – 20 mins. TEMPERATURE: E.425°F (220°C) G.7.
QUANTITIES for 12 tartlets

4 ozs hazel nuts (125 g)

Put the nuts in a baking tin and heat in a moderate oven until they are toasted and the skins come off easily. Cool and rub off as much loose skin as possible. Blend to chop them finely and tip into a bowl.

2 oz caster sugar (50 g): 3 Tbs water

Heat until the sugar dissolves and the syrup boils. Add the nuts.

2 Tbs chopped mixed peel

Add and mix well. Set aside to cool.

8 – 12 oz. short, flaky or puff pastry (250 – 375 g)

Roll out thinly and cut rounds to line small bun tins. Cut rounds for lids. Put a little of the filling in each, moisten the edges, cover with the lids and press well. Brush the tops with beaten egg or milk and bake until the pastry is lightly browned. Serve hot or cold.

LEMON FLAN FILLING

QUANTITIES for a 7 – 8 in. (18 – 20 cm) flan

2 lemons

Pare off the yellow rind and cut it in strips. If there is a lot of white pith, pare off some of this and discard it. Cut the lemons in four pieces and put them in the blender goblet with the rind, and water barely to cover. Blend until the rind is finely chopped. Strain if necessary and make up to ½ pt (250 ml) with water. Return to goblet.

1 oz custard powder (25 g): 2 – 3 oz sugar (50 – 75 g)

Add to the goblet and blend for a few seconds. Tip into a small pan, stir until it boils and simmer for one minute.

½ oz butter or margarine (1 Tbs): Cream (optional):

Add the fat and stir until it melts. Add cream at this stage. Pour into the flan case and leave to set. Garnish with

Fruit or Whipped cream

Alternative. Substitute 2 small oranges or 1 small grapefruit for the lemons.

LEMON AND ORANGE FLAN

QUANTITIES for an 8 in. (20 cm) flan

1 pt lemon jelly (½ l)

Make the jelly with only half the usual amount of water, dissolving it by blending a second or two with the hot water. Pour into a basin and stand this in a bowl of cold or iced water to cool until just beginning to set.

Recipe for Biscuit Flan page 124

Make the flan and put in the refrigerator to set.

¼ pt chilled evaporated milk (150 ml)

When the jelly is beginning to set put it in the blender goblet with the milk. Process for 30 seconds and pour it into the flan case. Leave to set.

Sliced fresh oranges or canned mandarin oranges

Decorate the top with fruit and keep it cold until ready to be served.

PEAR AND GINGER FLAN

QUANTITIES for a 7 – 8 in. (18 – 20 cm) flan, lined with biscuit crust or a short pastry baked blind.

1 lb 13 oz can of pears (750 g): ½ oz gelatine (1 ½ Tbs)

Drain the pears and reserve one half pear for garnishing. Boil the syrup to concentrate it to about ¼ pt (150 ml). Allow to go off the boil and then put in the blender goblet. Sprinkle in the gelatine and blend on slow speed for a few seconds. Add the pears cut in pieces and blend to a smooth purée.

2 pieces of ginger in syrup, cut up

Add to the goblet and blend just to chop the ginger. Turn into a bowl and leave to cool until it begins to thicken. Then spread it evenly in the flan case and put it in the refrigerator to finish setting.

Garnish the top with thin slices of pear and ginger. Serve with or without

Cream.

PUMPKIN FLAN OR PIE

It is very important that the pumpkin used for this should be a sunripened one, otherwise there is no pumpkin flavour in the finished flan. Canned pumpkin purée usually has a very good flavour and may be the better choice.

COOKING TIME: 45 mins. TEMPERATURE: E.400°F (200°C) G.6. QUANTITIES for a 7 in. (18 cm) flan.

Line the flan with short pastry and put it in the refrigerator to chill.

8 oz cooked and drained ripe pumpkin (250 g) or 8 oz canned pumpkin purée: ½ oz brown sugar (1 Tbs): 1 oz golden syrup (25 g): 1 tsp ground ginger: Pinch of grated nutmeg: Pinch of salt: 1 egg: ⅛ pt milk (60 ml)

Put all the ingredients in the blender goblet and mix smooth. Pour into the flan case and bake until set. Serve hot or cold.

PINEAPPLE FLAN

QUANTITIES for a 7 - 8 in. (18 – 20 cm) flan.

Make the flan case of short pastry and bake blind, or make a biscuit flan case.

About 15½ oz can of pineapple slices (375 g): 2 Tbs potato flour or arrowroot

Keep back one slice of pineapple for garnishing. Put the remainder, with the juice and potato flour, in the blender goblet and mix until smooth. Put in a pan and stir and heat until it comes to the boil. Remove from the heat.

½ oz butter (1 Tbs): 1 Tbs lemon juice: Sugar to taste

Add to the pineapple mixture and pour into the flan case. Sprinkle with caster sugar and leave to become cold.

Mandarin oranges or other canned or fresh fruit

Decorate the top of the flan with the pineapple ring cut in pieces and with other fruit to taste.

2 – 3 Tbs apricot jam: 2 – 3 Tbs warm water: A little kirsch

Blend until smooth and spoon over the fruit to glaze it. Leave to become cold.

Chapter Eighteen

HOT BAKED AND STEAMED PUDDINGS

Even if you have a mixer as well as a blender you may find it quicker to use the blender for making plain baked and steamed puddings.

Puddings based on bread crumbs or cake crumbs, like Queen of Puddings, can also be made in a fraction of the usual time.

If you prefer to use butcher's suet instead of the packet variety, the blender will do away with the messy business of grating the suet. Put the flour (6 oz or 150 g at a time), in the goblet. Add the suet broken in small pieces and with all the skin removed. Process on/off until the suet is finely chopped, a matter of a second or so.

BAKED BANANA MOUSSE

COOKING TIME: 30 – 40 mins. TEMPERATURE: E.375°F (190°C) G.5.

QUANTITIES for 4 – 6

1½ oz soft butter (40 g): 2 Tbs granulated sugar: 2 egg yolks: ¼ pt milk (150 ml): ¼ pt sherry (150 ml): 1 lb bananas (500 g)

Skin the bananas and cut them in pieces. Put all the ingredients in the goblet and blend until smooth.

2 egg whites

Beat until stiff and fold in the blended mixture. Pour into a well greased baking dish or soufflé dish, 2 – 3 pint size (1 – 1½ l). The dish should be not more than three-quarters full. Bake until the mixture is set. Serve plain or with single cream.

BAKED FRUIT SPONGE

COOKING TIME: ¾ – 1 hrs. TEMPERATURE: E.400°F (200°C) G.6.

QUANTITIES for a 1½ – 2 pt (1 l) piedish or other baking dish.

1 lb apples, plums, rhubarb or other fruit (500 g): 2 oz sugar or to taste (50 g)

Peel and slice apples, stone plums, cut the rhubarb in small pieces. Put the fruit in the baking dish, sprinkle with the sugar and cook until almost tender, about 20 minutes.

3 Tbs milk: 2 oz soft butter or margarine (50 g): 4 oz caster sugar (125 g): Vanilla or other flavouring: 1 egg

Put in the goblet and blend on high speed for 1 minute. Tip into a mixing bowl.

6 oz self-raising flour (150 g)

Add to the blended mixture and stir to combine the ingredients. Spread evenly over the hot fruit and bake until brown and set, about 20 minutes. Serve hot or cold with

Cream or Custard sauce.

BAKED SOUFFLÉ OMELET

COOKING TIME: 15 – 20 mins. TEMPERATURE: E.350°F (180°C) G.4.

QUANTITIES for 4; for a well-greased 2 pt (1 l) baking dish.

4 eggs

Separate the whites and yolks and put the yolks in the blender goblet. Beat the whites in a bowl until stiff.

2 Tbs caster sugar: Pinch of salt: 2 oz macaroons (50 g), broken: 1 tsp mixed chopped peel: 2 tsp potato flour or fecule

Add these to the yolks in the goblet and blend until mixture is thick and smooth. Tip it into the beaten whites and fold together. Pour into the prepared dish which should be not more than half full. Cook until the omelet is risen and brown. Serve at once, sprinkled with caster sugar. Serve separately

Single cream.

BANANA SOUFFLÉ

COOKING TIME: 30 – 35 mins. TEMPERATURE: E.375°F (190°C) G.5.

QUANTITIES for 3 – 4; for a well-greased 1 pt (½ l) soufflé dish

1 oz butter or margarine (25 g): 3 egg yolks: 8 oz bananas (250 g): 2 tsp lemon juice: 2 oz sugar (50 g): ¼ pt hot milk (150 ml)

Peel the bananas and cut in several pieces. Put all the ingredients in the goblet and blend until smooth. Pour into the saucepan and cook over a moderate heat, stirring all the time, until the mixture thickens. Remove from the heat.

3 egg whites

Beat until stiff and fold into the banana mixture. Put in the prepared soufflé dish and bake until risen and lightly browned. Serve at once with

Cream, or a lemon or fruit sauce.

HAZEL NUT SOUFFLÉ

COOKING TIME: 20 – 30 mins. TEMPERATURE: E.375°F (190°C) G.5.

QUANTITIES for a 1½ pt soufflé or other baking dish (1 l) well greased.

3 oz toasted hazel nuts (75 g): 2 oz caster sugar (50 g): 1 oz butter or margarine (25 g): ¼ pt hot milk (150 ml): 3 egg yolks

To toast the nuts, cook them in a moderate oven until they begin to brown. There is no need to rub off the skins for this soufflé. Blend all the ingredients until the nuts are finely chopped. Return to the pan and stir vigorously until the mixture thickens. Remove from the heat.

3 egg whites

Beat until stiff. Add the nut mixture and fold together carefully. Put in the prepared dish and bake until well risen and lightly browned. It should still be soft in the centre.

Serve at once, plain or with

Single cream or a thin chocolate sauce.

LEMON DELICIOUS PUDDING

COOKING TIME: 45 mins. TEMPERATURE: E.350°F (180°C) G.4.
QUANTITIES for 3 – 4

1 strip of yellow rind: 2 Tbs lemon juice: 5 oz sugar (150 g):
2 Tbs flour: 2 egg yolks: ¼ pt milk (150 ml): 2 tsp soft butter

Put all in the goblet and blend for 1 minute to mix well and chop the lemon rind finely.

2 egg whites

Beat stiffly and add the lemon mixture. Fold together. Pour into a greased baking dish and cook until set. This pudding separates into two layers during cooking. Serve warm or cold.

QUEEN OF PUDDINGS

COOKING TIME: 1 hr. TEMPERATURE: E.350°F (180°C) G.4.
QUANTITIES for 4 – 6

4 oz bread (125 g)

Remove the crusts and tear the bread in pieces. Drop the pieces through the open top of the goblet with the motor running at slow speed. Blend to fine crumbs and tip into a basin. In a small blender this may need to be done in two lots.

1 pt hot milk (½ l): ½ oz butter (1 Tbs): 1 oz sugar (25 g):
Pinch salt: 2 egg yolks: ½ tsp vanilla essence, or a strip of yellow
lemon rind

Put in the goblet and mix well. Pour over the crumbs and combine. Put in an oiled baking dish and cook until the pudding is set in the middle, about ½ hr. Remove from the oven and leave to stand while the meringue is prepared.

2 – 3 oz soft jam (2 – 3 Tbs): 2 egg whites: 3 oz sugar (75 g)

Whip the egg whites until stiff enough to stand up in peaks. Fold in the sugar. Spread the jam on top of the pudding and pile the meringue on top. Bake until the meringue begins to colour, about 15 mins. Serve hot or cold.

STEAMED TREACLE PUDDING

COOKING TIME: 2 hrs. QUANTITIES for 4 – 6

4 oz caster sugar (125 g): 4 oz soft butter or margarine (125 g): 2 eggs: 8 oz black treacle (250 g): 4 Tbs milk

Put all in the goblet and blend for 1 minute. Tip into a mixing bowl.

8 oz self-raising flour (250 g)

Add to the blended mixture and combine carefully. Pour into a greased 1½ pint (1 l) pudding basin, cover with foil, and steam. Turn out and serve with

Custard sauce or cream.

STEAMED MARMALADE SPONGE

COOKING TIME: 1 – 1½ hrs. QUANTITIES for 4

4 Tbs marmalade

Grease a 1½ pint (1 l) pudding basin and put the marmalade in the bottom.

3 Tbs milk: 2 oz soft butter or margarine (50 g): 4 oz caster sugar (125 g): Lemon essence or strips of lemon rind: 1 egg

Put in the goblet and blend for 1 minute. Tip into a mixing bowl.

6 oz self-raising flour (150 g)

Add to the bowl and stir to combine the ingredients. Put in the prepared basin, cover with foil and steam.

4 Tbs marmalade: 4 Tbs water

Blend to make smooth and heat for a sauce to pour over the pudding when it is turned out.

Alternative. Make the pudding in four individual moulds and steam for ¾ hour.

STEAMED JAM LAYER PUDDING

COOKING TIME: 2 hrs. QUANTITIES for 4

8 oz self-raising flour (250 g): ¼ tsp salt: 4 oz butcher's suet (125 g): ¼ pt water (150 ml)

Break or cut the suet in small pieces, removing as much membrane as possible. Blend it in two lots with half the flour and salt each time. Blend to chop the suet, only a second or so being needed. Tip into a bowl and mix to a soft dough with water. Divide the pastry into four pieces. Roll one to fit the bottom of a greased 1 pint (½ l) basin.

8 oz jam or marmalade (250 g)

Spread a layer of jam on the pastry. Roll each of the other pieces a little bigger than the last and layer them with jam, finishing with pastry. Cover the top of the basin with foil and place the pudding in a pan with boiling water coming half way up the side of the basin. Boil the water steadily for 2 hours, topping up with boiling water as necessary. Remove the pudding, take off the lid and leave to stand for 5 minutes before turning out on a hot dish. Serve plain or with cream or custard sauce.

Chapter Nineteen

QUICK BREADS AND COFFEE CAKES

Quick breads are useful for tea-time (less sweet and rich than cakes), for high teas, with morning coffee, or for a continental-type breakfast. The "coffee" cakes are plain cake mixtures baked with a nutty or fruit topping, a type of cake popular in Europe and America where they are also made with a rich yeast dough as the base.

The quick breads are meant to be sliced and buttered though they are most of them very good eaten plain.

BANANA BREAD

COOKING TIME: 1 hr. TEMPERATURE: E.350°F (180°C) G.4.
QUANTITIES for a 1 lb (500 g) loaf

4 oz self-raising flour (125 g): ½ tsp salt

Put in a mixing bowl.

2 oz shelled nuts (50 g)

Put in the goblet and blend at slow speed to chop them. Add to the flour.

1 oz soft margarine (25 g): 3 Tbs golden syrup: 1 egg: 8 oz bananas (250 g)

Skin the bananas and cut them in pieces. Put them in the goblet with the other ingredients and blend until smooth. Add to the dry ingredients and combine well. Put in the well-oiled loaf tin and bake until firm in the centre. Turn out on a rack to cool. When quite cold store in a polythene bag or box for 24 hours before cutting.

CHEESE LOAF

COOKING TIME: 1 hr. TEMPERATURE: E.350°F (180°C) G.4.
QUANTITIES for a 1 lb loaf tin (500 g)

8 oz self-raising flour (250 g): ½ tsp salt

Put these in a mixing bowl.

1 egg: Approximately ¼ pt milk (150 ml): 3 oz well-flavoured cheese, cut in pieces (75 g)

Put these in the blender goblet and mix until smooth. Pour into the flour and combine well, adding more milk if needed to make the mixture a stiff cake consistency. Put in the well-oiled tin and bake until light brown and firm in the centre. Turn out on a rack to cool. Unlike most of the other loaves, this one can be sliced as soon as it is cold, or even before.

COFFEE CAKE

COOKING TIME: 30 mins. TEMPERATURE: E.400°F (200°C) G.6.
QUANTITIES for an 8 in. (20 cm) sandwich tin

Use a tin with a false bottom or line a tin with foil. Grease the tin.

2 oz shelled walnuts (50 g)

Blend on slow speed to chop coarsely. Tip into a small bowl.

*1 oz melted butter or margarine (25 g): ½ tsp grated nutmeg:
3 oz light brown sugar (75 g): 1 tsp cinnamon*

Mix these into the nuts and set aside to cool.

*3 Tbs milk: 2 oz soft butter or margarine (50 g): 4 oz caster
sugar (125 g): Vanilla or other flavouring: 1 egg*

The milk and egg should be at room temperature. Put all the ingredients in the goblet and blend at high speed for 1 minute. Tip into a mixing bowl.

6 oz self-raising flour (150 g)

Add to the blended mixture and stir to combine. Spread evenly in the prepared tin and sprinkle the nut topping over the surface. Bake until firm in the centre. Lift the cake out onto a rack to cool, being careful to keep it upright. Serve warm or cold.

ORANGE LOAF

COOKING TIME: 1 hr. TEMPERATURE: E.350°F (180°C) G.4.
QUANTITIES for a 1 lb loaf tin (500 g)

8 oz self-raising flour (250 g): ½ tsp salt

Put these in a mixing bowl.

*¼ pt milk (150 ml): 1 Tbs honey: 1 egg: 1 small orange: 1 oz
soft margarine (25 g)*

Wash the orange and squeeze out the juice. Put this in the goblet with the other ingredients. Cut the orange shell in pieces and add it. Blend to chop the peel finely.

2 oz stoned dates (50 g)

Cut the dates in pieces and add to the orange mixture. Blend just to chop the dates. Pour this into the flour and mix together. Put in the well-oiled tin and bake until lightly browned and firm in the centre. Turn out on a rack to cool, and when quite cold, store in a polythene bag for 24 hours before cutting.

SPICY FRUIT LOAF
(can also be used as a plain cake)

COOKING TIME: 1½ hrs. TEMPERATURE: E.325°F (160°C) G.3.
QUANTITIES for a 2 lb loaf tin (1 kg), or a 7 in. cake tin (18 cm);

Grease tin and line bottom with paper.

10 oz self-raising flour (300 g): 4 oz sultanas (125 g)

Put these in a mixing bowl.

1 oz shelled walnuts (25 g)

Put in the blender and process on slow speed to chop them. Add to the flour.

2 oz soft butter or margarine (50 g): 1 egg: ¼ pt milk (150 ml): ½ tsp cinnamon: ¼ tsp ginger: 4 Tbs black treacle: 4 oz caster sugar (125 g)

Put all in the goblet and blend for 1 minute. Add to the flour mixture and combine thoroughly. Put in the prepared tin and bake. Turn out on a rack to cool. When quite cold, store in a polythene bag for 24 hours before cutting.

TREACLE AND NUT LOAF

COOKING TIME: 1 – 1¼ hrs. TEMPERATURE: E.350°F (180°C) G.4.
QUANTITIES for a 1 lb loaf tin (500 g), or a 6 in. cake tin (15 cm)

8 oz self-raising flour (250 g):

Put in a mixing bowl.

2 oz shelled walnuts (50 g)

Put in the blender goblet and process at slow speed to chop them. Add to the flour.

1 egg: ¼ pt milk (150 ml): 2 oz fine brown sugar (50 g): 4 Tbs black treacle

Put in the goblet and blend for a few seconds.

137

2 oz stoned dates (50 g)

Cut the dates in half and add to the ingredients in the goblet. Blend to chop the dates. Pour into the flour and mix together. Put in the tin which has been heavily oiled or lined with non-stick paper. Bake until firm in the centre. Turn out on a rack and allow to become quite cold before storing in a polythene bag. Keep for 24 hours before slicing.

WHEATEN DATE LOAF

This makes a loaf of a close, firm texture, rather like a dark rye loaf, very delicious with butter for tea.

COOKING TIME: 1 hr. TEMPERATURE: E.350°F (180°C) G.4. QUANTITIES for a 7 in. cake tin (18 cm), well-oiled.

8 oz of 100% wholemeal flour (250 g): 4 oz plain white flour (125 g)

Mix these in a bowl.

¼ pt milk (150 ml): ½ tsp salt: 2 Tbs black treacle: 1 tsp cream of tartar: 1 tsp bicarbonate of soda: 4 oz stoned, sliced dates (125 g)

Put in the goblet and blend to mix and chop the dates. Add to the flour together with enough more milk (about ¼ pt) to make a soft consistency. Put in the tin and spread the top evenly. Bake until firm in the centre. Turn out on a rack to cool and, when quite cold, store in a polythene bag for 24 hours before cutting thinly.

Chapter Twenty

CAKES, BISCUITS AND ICINGS

The blender has limited uses in this branch of cookery and most cakes are better if mixed by hand or in a mixing machine, though some blender manufacturers recommend using their models for conventional cake making. In this case the fat, eggs and sugar are blended until light and fluffy, then tipped into a mixing bowl and the other ingredients added and mixed in by hand or machine. For good results the eggs and fat must be at room temperature.

The cakes I find most useful to blend are those like gingerbreads and honey cakes, where the sugar, fat and syrup are normally melted together. The saucepan can be dispensed with if the blender is used.

I also use the blender a great deal for making cakes containing nuts and have included sereval recipes for these, mostly of continental origin.

ALMOND MACAROONS

COOKING TIME: 30 – 40 mins. TEMPERATURE: E.325°F (160°C) G.3.
QUANTITIES for 18 macaroons

6 oz almonds (150 g)

Blanch the almonds by pouring boiling water over them. Leave a few minutes, strain and add cold water. Remove the skins and dry the nuts on a paper kitchen towel. Put them in the goblet in one or two lots and blend until finely ground. Tip into a bowl.

8 oz caster sugar (250 g): 1 Tbs ground rice: Pinch salt

Add to the almonds.

2 egg whites

Put in the goblet and blend just to break them up well. Add to the other ingredients and mix well. Roll the mixture in balls in the palms of the hands, flatten and put on heavily greased baking trays or on non-stick paper.

18 blanched almonds (optional)

Press an almond on each macaroon and bake until they are firm and a pale biscuit colour. Cool on a rack and store in an airtight box.

AUSTRIAN HAZEL NUT GÂTEAU

COOKING TIME: 40 mins. TEMPERATURE: E.375°F (190°C) G.5.
QUANTITIES for a 7 in. (18 cm) cake tin.

Grease the tin and dust it with flour, or line the bottom with non-stick paper.

8 oz shelled hazel nuts (250 g)

Toast the nuts by baking them in a moderate oven until the skins will rub off easily, though this is merely used as a test for the toasting and skins are left on for this cake. Cool the nuts. Put them in the goblet in two or more lots and blend on slow speed to chop coarsely. On/off is usually sufficient. Tip them into a bowl.

3 egg yolks: 6 oz caster sugar (150 g): 1 Tbs rum

Put in the goblet and blend until thick and light.

3 egg whites

Beat until stiff and standing in peaks. Fold in the nuts and egg yolk mixture and turn the mixture into the prepared tin. Bake until lightly browned. Invert the tin over a cake rack and turn out gently. Leave until cold.

Butter cream or whipped cream

When quite cold, slice the cake through the middle and fill it with whipped cream or butter cream flavoured with rum, vanilla or finely ground toasted hazel nuts. Ice if desired. Coffee-flavoured filling and icing goes well with this cake.

HAZEL NUT COOKIES

COOKING TIME: 20 mins. TEMPERATURE: E.350°F (180°C) G.4.
QUANTITIES for 12 cookies

4 oz shelled hazel nuts (125 g)

Toast the nuts in a moderate oven until they are lightly browned and the skins rub off easily. Cool and rub off the skins. Put the nuts in the goblet and blend at slow speed to grind to a coarse powder. Tip into a bowl.

1 egg white: 2 oz granulated sugar (50 g): ½ tsp vanilla

Put in the goblet and blend to mix thoroughly. Add to the nuts and mix well. Roll into balls or put small spoonsful on non-stick paper or foil on a baking tray. Decorate with an untoasted nut. Bake until lightly browned and leave on the trays to finish drying and become firm. When they are quite cold, store them in an airtight container.

AUSTRIAN WALNUT GÂTEAU

COOKING TIME: 40 mins. TEMPERATURE: E.375°F (190°C) G.5.
QUANTITIES for a 7 in (18 cm) deep sandwich tin or cake tin.

Grease the tin and dust it with flour, or line the bottom with non-stick paper.

1 oz dry bread, without crusts (25 g): 3 oz shelled walnuts (75 g)

Tear the bread in small pieces, put in the goblet and blend at slow speed to make fine crumbs. Tip into a bowl. Put the nuts in the goblet and blend on slow speed just to chop them coarsely. Add to the crumbs.

3 egg yolks: 1 Tbs rum or 1 tsp vanilla: 3 oz caster sugar (75 g)

Put in the goblet and blend until thick and light. Tip into a mixing bowl.

3 egg whites

Beat the egg whites until stiff enough to stand up in peaks. Add the nut and crumb mixture alternately with the egg yolk mixture and fold into the whites carefully. Put into the prepared tin, smooth the top and bake until firm in the centre. Turn out on a rack to cool.

Butter cream or Whipped cream; Icing, optional

When the cake is cold, split it in half and fill as desired. Coffee or chocolate fillings and icings are very good with the walnut flavour.

HAZEL NUT BISCUITS

COOKING TIME: 15 – 20 mins. TEMPERATURE: E.350°F (180°C) G.4.

QUANTITIES for 24 biscuits 2½ in. (5 cm) diameter.

4 oz hazel nuts (125 g): 1 oz unblanched almonds (25 g)

Blend finely, on slow speed in one or two lots. Tip into a mixing bowl.

6 oz caster sugar (150 g)

Add to the nuts.

2 egg whites

Blend to break up well and add to the nuts and sugar. Mix well.

about 3 oz plain flour (75 g)

Stir in enough flour to make a stiff consistency suitable for rolling out. Roll ¼ inch (½ cm) thick and cut in rounds with a fluted cutter. Put on heavily greased baking tins or put pieces of non-stick paper on the tins. Bake until the biscuits are lightly browned and firm.

Serve plain for tea or with light fruit sweets or ices.

Alternative. Decorate with chocolate icing and chopped hazel nuts.

GINGERBREAD

COOKING TIME: 45 – 50 mins. TEMPERATURE: E.350°F (180°C) G.4.

QUANTITIES for an 8 – 9 in. (20 – 24 cm) square tin or a similar capacity shallow baking tin. Grease the tin and line the bottom with non-stick paper.

¼ pt milk (150 ml): ½ tsp mixed spice: 1½ oz brown sugar (3 Tbs): 1½ tsp ground ginger: 8 oz golden syrup (250 g): ½ tsp bicarbonate of soda: 1 egg: 4 oz soft butter or margarine (125 g)

Put all the ingredients in the goblet, first cutting the fat in pieces. Blend for 1 minute or until smooth and light. Tip into a mixing bowl.

4 oz plain white flour (125 g): 4 oz wholemeal flour (125 g): 1 oz chopped peel or preserved ginger (25 g): 2 oz sultanas (50 g): Pinch of salt

Add to the blended mixture and stir until well combined. Pour into the prepared tin and bake until it feels springy in the middle and begins to shrink from the sides of the tin. Turn out on a rack and leave to cool. Store for a day or so before using.

LITTLE CUPIDS

COOKING TIME: 15 – 20 mins. for the pastry shells.
QUANTITIES for 12 or more tarts made in bun tins.

Use a good short pastry to make the little tarts and bake them blind. Use 4 – 6 oz flour (125 – 150 g) for the pastry. Bake at 425°F (220°C) G.7. Cool before filling.

4 oz macaroons or ratafia biscuits (125 g)

Break in pieces and put in the goblet. Blend on/off until reduced to fine crumbs. Tip into a small basin.

3 Tbs sherry or brandy

Add to the crumbs and leave to soak.

¼ pt whipping cream (150 ml): Glacé cherries and angelica

Whip the cream until stiff but not buttery. Stir in the crumb mixture. Put in the tart shells and garnish with cherries and angelica or other garnish to taste. Keep cold until required.

PRALINE

(for flavouring butter creams, ices, soufflés, omelets etc.)

3 oz caster sugar (75 g): 3 oz unblanched almonds (75 g)

Put in a small pan and heat slowly until the sugar melts and begins to colour. Stir well and continue cooking until the sugar is nut-brown in colour. Turn the mixture onto an oiled baking tin and leave it to become quite cold. Break it up into small pieces, (one-almond size), put in the blender in one or two lots and blend at slow speed until it is a fine powder. Put this in an airtight container and store it in a dry place.

Alternative. Instead of making the praline, buy almond toffee and blend it to a powder. This is not quite the same because the almonds are usually blanched and there is more toffee and less almond than with the home-made variety.

PRALINE CAKE

Make a genoese sponge mixture in two 8 in. (20 cm) sandwich tins. When the cake is cold, split to make a total of 4 layers. Use the praline variation of the Butter Cream recipe page 145 to join the layers together. The top can be iced with the same cream or simply sprinkled with finely crushed praline. If it is iced, sprinkle the top with blender-chopped roasted almonds.

REFRIGERATED FRUIT CAKE
(uncooked)

QUANTITIES for 4 – 6

4 oz gingernuts (125 g): 2 oz shellled nuts (50 g)

Break the gingernuts in small pieces and blend them on low speed to make crumbs. Tip out into a bowl and blend the nuts to chop them. Add to the crumbs.

2 oz marshmallows (50 g): 2 Tbs fruit juice: 2 oz stoned and sliced dates (50 g): 1 tsp brandy: Pinch salt: ½ tsp cinnamon

Use kitchen scissors to cut the marshmallows into small pieces and put them in the blender with the other ingredients. Blend until well broken up. Add to the crumbs and nuts.

2 oz seedless raisins (50 g): 2 oz glacé cherries (50 g): 2 oz chopped mixed peel (50 g): 2 oz currants (50 g)

Cut the cherries in quarters and add the fruit to the bowl of ingredients. Mix together thoroughly and pack in a freezer tray or similar container lined with foil or non-stick lining paper. Refrigerate in the ice compartment for not less than 12 hours, with the top of the cake covered with paper or foil.

Whipped cream

Turn out on a serving dish and use as a cake or pudding, served with cream.

SWISS HONEY CAKE

COOKING TIME: 30 mins. TEMPERATURE: E. 350°F (180°C) G.4.
QUANTITIES for a Swiss roll tin about 13 in. × 9 in. (33 × 23 cm)

Line the tin with non-stick paper or foil having the sides project about an inch above the edges of the tin.

4 oz blanched almonds (125 g)

Put half the almonds in the goblet and blend at slow speed to make a fine meal. Add remaining almonds and blend just enough to chop them. Tip into a mixing bowl.

8 oz self-raising flour (250 g): 1 oz chopped mixed peel (25 g): 8 oz caster sugar (250 g)

Add to the almonds

6 oz honey (150 g): 1 tsp cinnamon: ½ tsp mixed spice: 1 egg

Put in the blender goblet and mix smooth. Add to the dry ingredients and mix to a stiff dough. Roll, or pat out to fit the baking tin, smoothing the top with a knife. Bake until the centre feels set. Turn out on a rack and leave to become cold.

Lemon glacé icing, see page 146 using 6 – 8 oz icing sugar (150 – 250 g)

Ice the top of the cake thinly, leave to set and then store the cake for about three days to allow it to soften before cutting it into fingers or squares. It is very sweet and small pieces are enough. It keeps very well in a tin or polythene box.

UNCOOKED CHOCOLATE CAKE

QUANTITIES for an 8 in. (20 cm) flan or sandwich tin.

Put the flan ring on a flat plate or line the tin with foil.

6 oz semi-sweet biscuits (150 g): 2 oz shelled walnuts (50 g)

Break the biscuits in pieces and blend them in several lots to make coarse crumbs. Tip into a mixing bowl. Blend the nuts to chop them coarsely. Add to the crumbs.

3 oz butter or margarine (75 g): 2 oz fine brown sugar (50 g):
3 Tbs golden syrup or honey: 2 oz cocoa powder (50 g): Vanilla
or rum

Put in a small pan and stir and heat until the fat melts and the mixture just boils. Pour over the crumb mixture. Combine thoroughly and press into the prepared tin, spreading the top flat with a knife. Leave overnight before removing the flan ring or foil and icing with

Chocolate or mocha icing

Decorate the cake to taste and cut in small wedges for serving.

BUTTER CREAM

1 oz custard powder (3 Tbs) :1½ oz sugar (3 Tbs): ½ pt milk
(250 ml)

Put in the blender goblet and mix smooth. Pour into a pan and stir until boiling. Simmer for 2 – 3 minutes. Stand the pan in cold water until the custard has cooled to luke warm. Return it to the blender.

4 oz soft butter or margarine (125 g): Flavouring

Add half the fat and mix on slow speed for a few seconds. Add the rest of the fat and the flavouring and blend until smooth. Tip into a dish, cover, and refrigerate until firm.

Flavourings:
1. Add 2 oz crushed praline, see page 143.
2. Break 2 oz plain chocolate in pieces and melt it in the hot sauce, after it has been cooked.
3. Add soluble coffee to taste.
4. Add 2 Tbs nuts, blended finely.
5. Add a strip of yellow orange or lemon rind to the first three

ingredients when they are being blended, blend to chop the peel finely.

Alternative. For a firmer cream, dissolve $\frac{1}{2}$ Tbs gelatine in 1 Tbs hot water and add at the same time as the fat.

GLACÉ ICING

QUANTITIES: Sufficient for icing the top of two 8 in. (20 cm) cakes.

8 oz icing sugar (250 g): 2 Tbs hot water: Flavouring and colouring

Put the ingredients in the goblet and blend on slow speed until smooth. Pour at once onto the cake and allow to spread, possibly helping it with a knife dipped in hot water. Should the icing be left in the goblet until it has thickened, add more water and blend for a second.

Flavourings:
1. Use essences or liqueurs to taste, reducing the amount of water as necessary.
2. Substitute 3 – 4 Tbs lemon or orange juice for the water.
3. Add 3 Tbs cocoa powder and increase the water to 3 Tbs. Add a small knob of butter or margarine to give the icing a shine.
4. Add 1 tsp or more of soluble coffee and a small knob of butter or margarine.

MOCHA BUTTER ICING

2 oz soft butter or margarine (50 g): 4 Tbs boiling water: 2 tsp instant coffee

Put in the goblet and blend on slow speed until well mixed.

3 Tbs cocoa: Pinch of salt: 4 oz icing sugar (125 g)

Add and blend on high speed, scraping down as necessary. Blend to mix well.

4 oz icing sugar (125 g)

Add and blend at slow speed until well mixed. If the icing is to be poured over a cake use it straight from the goblet and use at once; otherwise tip it into a bowl and leave to become firm, before spreading it in the usual way.

Chapter Twenty-one

PRESERVES AND BLENDING
FOR THE HOME FREEZER

Blending the ingredients for jams, marmalades and chutneys speeds up the cooking and gives a better flavour to the finished product. It also makes it a practical proposition to prepare just small amounts of a preserve as required.

Jams
The blender makes smooth, pulpy jams, like the old conserves or butters. They are excellent for spreading and for all cooking purposes.

Marmalade
If the fruit is chopped in the blender before it is cooked, a blender marmalade will be similar to that made when a mincer is used to chop the peel. Use any recipe requiring chopped or sliced peel. To chop it in the blender, peel the fruit and cut the rinds in strips. Cover them with some of the water in the recipe and blend on high speed until they are chopped as required; on/off may be sufficient. Finish the making in the usual way.

Blending after the fruit has been cooked produces a thick, smooth marmalade ideal for spreading and for all cooking purposes. Those who like a thick fruity marmalade but who can't manage bits of peel will appreciate this kind. If a pressure cooker is available this kind of marmalade can be made in an hour, from start to finish, see the first two recipes.

Chutney
With most modern recipes the vegetables and fruit are minced before being cooked to a pulp. Chopping in the blender is quicker than mincing and is suitable for all vegetables and fruit. Prepare them in the usual way and cut them in large pieces for the blender.

For firm vegetables, put them in the goblet with cold water to cover. Blend long enough to chop finely, strain and proceed with the recipe. Soft vegetables, fruit and tomatoes can be chopped dry or with a little of the vinegar in the recipe.

THICK SEVILLE ORANGE MARMALADE

QUANTITIES for 5 lb (2½ kg)

1½ lb Seville oranges (¾ kg): 1½ pt water (750 ml)

Wash the oranges and put them in a pressure cooker with the water. Cover and pressure cook for 20 minutes at 15 lb pressure. Reduce the pressure slowly at room temperature. When the oranges are cool enough to handle cut them in half, remove pips and put the oranges in the blender goblet in several lots according to the capacity of the goblet. Blend until smooth. Put in the preserving pan or large saucepan.

Juice of 1 lemon (2 Tbs): 3 lb granulated sugar (1½ kg)

Add to the oranges and heat and stir until the sugar dissolves and the marmalade boils. Boil rapidly until a little sets when tested in the usual way. Drop a little on a cold saucer, leave a few minutes and push with the finger to see if the surface wrinkles, indicating it is done. Pot and seal in the usual way.

QUICK LEMON MARMALADE

QUANTITIES for 5 lb (2½ kg)

1½ lb lemons (750 g): 1½ pt water (750 ml)

Wash the lemons thoroughly and pressure cook them with the water for 15 minutes at 15 lb pressure. Allow the pressure to drop slowly. Remove the fruit and leave it to cool until it can be handled. Cut the lemons in half, remove the pips and blend the fruit in two or more lots depending on the capacity of the goblet. Use some of the cooking water if needed during blending. Tip into the preserving pan or large saucepan.

3 lb granulated sugar (1½ kg)

Add sugar, stir until the marmalade boils and then boil rapidly until setting point is reached, see previous recipe. Pot and seal in the usual way.

SWEET ORANGE MARMALADE

This recipe makes a really orange-coloured marmalade with a fresh orange flavour, similar to the marmalades of Spain. It is excellent on bread and for giving a fresh fruit flavour to tarts and puddings.

QUANTITIES for 5 lb (2½ kg)

2 lb sweet oranges (1 kg): 2 pt water (1 l)

Wash the oranges and cut them into small pieces, removing the pips. Blend the oranges in several lots using some of the water each time. Blend to mince the fruit finely. It is better not to attempt to process too much at a time as some of it is then inclined to become pulpy before the rest is chopped. As soon as the top layer blends down it is usually chopped enough. Boil the fruit and water for 30 minutes or until the peel is just tender.

3 lb sugar (1½ kg): Juice of 2 lemons or 4 – 5 Tbs

Add to the fruit and stir until the sugar dissolves. Boil until setting point is reached. Pour into hot jars and cover at once or when quite cold.

Alternative. If you want to turn the recipe into a traditional type of English marmalade, soak the minced peel and water overnight and then boil for 1½ – 2 hours before adding the sugar. Add another pint of water for soaking and boiling as the longer cooking the peel has will cause more evaporation.

PLUM CONSERVE

COOKING TIME: 20 – 25 minutes. QUANTITIES for 3 lb (1½ kg)

2 lb plums (1 kg): 2 lb granulated sugar (1 kg)

Remove the stones and cut up the fruit. Blend it in two or more lots at high speed until it forms a purée. Take off the top of the goblet and gradually add the sugar, blending for 1 minute. Tip into a pan, bring to the boil, stirring frequently, and simmer gently for 20 – 25 minutes. Pour into small hot pots and either seal while hot or allow to become completely cold before sealing.

STRAWBERRY CONSERVE

This makes a smooth, thick preserve with a very good flavour, ideal for sweet sauces and many other cooking purposes.

QUANTITIES for 2½ lb (just over 1 kg)

2 lb strawberries (1 kg): 2 lb granulated sugar (1 kg)

Wash the fruit and remove the hulls. Blend in two or more lots for just long enough to make a purée. Tip into a pan and add the sugar. Stir until boiling and boil hard for 10 minutes or until the quantity is reduced to 2½ lb or just over 1 kg. Pour into small hot jars and seal at once, or when quite cold.

BLENDING FOR THE HOME FREEZER

Apart from using the blender to prepare fruit and vegetables for freezing, many other foods can be prepared in bulk and preserved in the freezer ready for immediate use. Although the blender prepares food so rapidly that advance preparation for freezer storage may seem unnecessary, yet there is always some preparation involved in preparing food for blending and to do a lot at a time and freeze the surplus is time-saving.

Most of the recipes in this book are suitable for freezer storage, particularly useful being the pâtés and spreads, sauces (except mayonnaise), quick breads, cakes, pancakes, biscuits and flan cases to be filled with the quickly blended quiche and flan mixtures.

Freezing Fruit Purées or Pulps

The most useful to preserve are apple, plum and damson, strawberries and other berries, for use in making cold sweets or sauces. It is a particularly good way of preserving very ripe or damaged fruit whether from the garden or the greengrocer.

Wash and prepare the fruit as for cooking. For a raw purée blend without any liquid, though sugar may be added. It is useful, though, to have some unsweetened. Berries may need to be strained to remove any remaining pips. Berries and soft stone fruits to be cooked, wash, then remove stones and heat the fruit slowly, without any water, until the juice begins to flow. Then blend with or without sugar. For hard fruits like apples, cook until tender before pulping.

Be careful not to over-blend as this mixes a lot of air with the fruit. If this happens, tap the containers in which you have put the purée to release the air before sealing.

When you have any left-over stewed fruit, or have opened a larger can of fruit than required, it is a good plan to purée the surplus and freeze it for use later.

Freezing Vegetable Purées

Purées of single or mixed vegetables are very useful to store for making soups or for serving with meat and other savoury dishes. There are a number of vegetable purée recipes in the chapter on vegetables and these can be frozen, though where potato is included in the recipe it is better to freeze without it and add the potato powder to the re-heated vegetable.

To prepare purées for freezing, cook the vegetables in the usual way, blend smooth and pack in small containers. Shake or tap the container to remove air bubbles before sealing and freezing.

To heat the frozen purée put in a double boiler, in a basin over boiling water, or in a covered dish in the oven.

Chapter Twenty-Two

DRINKS

One of the most obvious uses for a blender is in mixing drinks of infinite variety.

Those who like cocktails can use the blender in place of a cocktail shaker, adding small ice cubes or roughly broken larger cubes, during blending.

The concentrated frozen or bottled juices can be blended with water and ice for quick refreshing fruit drinks of good flavour.

Dried milk can be mixed in it, but process for the minimum time or a lot of fairly stable froth will be produced and can be troublesome to get rid of. If hot milk for coffee has boiled and formed a skin, blend it back into the milk.

Cold or hot instant coffee and chocolate and proprietary drinks are all improved by a few seconds in the blender.

Whole fruits plus liquids can be made into drinks, including citrus fruits, berries, raw apples, bananas and most others.

SUGAR SYRUP

Make a supply of this to keep in the refrigerator for sweetening drinks, fruit salad and many other purposes.

QUANTITIES for ¾ pt (400 ml)

8 oz granulated sugar (250 g): ½ pt cold water (250 ml)

Blend until the sugar has dissolved, about 1 minute. The mixture clouds during blending but soon clears on standing.

FRUIT DRINKS

LEMONADE

2 medium-sized thin-skinned lemons: 1¼ pt cold water (750 ml): 2 oz sugar (50 g) or 2 Tbs honey or use the ready-made sugar syrup to sweeten to taste, see previous recipe

Wash the lemons and cut them in pieces or leave whole according to the type of blender. Very large, powerful ones will take whole lemons, others need to have them cut in pieces or slices. Put the fruit in the goblet with some or all of the water. Sugar or honey may be added at this stage, or after straining. Blend just to chop the lemons coarsely. Strain. Sweeten if not already done. Serve with ice cubes or chill in the refrigerator before serving.

If preferred, some of the water in the recipe can be replaced by crushed ice or ice cubes, added during blending.

ORANGEADE No. 1

QUANTITIES for 1 large glass or 2 small

Peel 1 small orange, slice it and remove the pips. Put it in the goblet, cover with cold water and blend for a few seconds. It can be served as it is or strained. For a sweet drink add sugar or sugar syrup to taste, see previous page.

ORANGEADE No. 2

QUANTITIES for 4 – 6 glasses

2 medium thin-skinned oranges or 1 orange and 1 lemon: 1 – 2 oz sugar (25 – 50 g): 1 pt cold water (500 ml)

Wash the fruit thoroughly. Cut it in small pieces and put it in the goblet with the water and sugar. Blend for a few seconds, just to break up the skins coarsely. Strain at once.

This method produces a very good flavour and colour without bitterness. Over-blending or using very thick-skinned fruit will make it bitter.

APPLE AND ORANGE DRINK

QUANTITIES for 4

Juice of 3 oranges: 4 dessert apples: 1 tsp lemon juice: 3 tsp sugar

Peel and core the apples and cut them in small pieces. Put all the ingredients in the goblet and blend for 1 minute. Serve with ice cubes or chill before serving. Stir before pouring into glasses as the top layer tends to turn brown on standing.

CARROT AND ORANGE COCKTAIL

QUANTITIES for 1 – 2 glasses

1 small orange: 2 oz carrot (50 g): 1 slice lemon

Peel and slice the orange. Scrape and dice the carrot. Put in the goblet with cold water to cover and blend for $\frac{1}{2}$ – 1 minute. Strain if desired. Chill before serving or serve with ice.

GRAPEFRUIT AND ORANGE DRINK

QUANTITIES for 1½ – 2 pints (1 l)

1 medium-sized grapefruit

If the grapefruit is a thin-skinned one simply wash it and cut in pieces. If the skin is thick, peel off the outside yellow rind and put in the blender goblet. Remove the white pith and discard it. Cut the rest of the fruit in pieces and put it in the goblet.

1 pt water ($\frac{1}{2}$ l): 4 oz sugar (125 g)

Add to the goblet and blend for a few seconds. Strain.

1 orange: $\frac{1}{2}$ pt water (250 ml)

Wash and cut up the orange and blend it with the water for a few seconds. Strain and add to the first juice. Chill before serving.

If your blender is a large one both the fruits can be blended together.

MILK, YOGURT AND COTTAGE CHEESE DRINKS

BANANA AND PINEAPPLE

QUANTITIES for 1 – 2 glasses.

1 small ripe banana: ¼ pt pineapple juice (150 ml): 1 heaped Tbs skimmed milk powder

Peel the banana and cut it in several pieces. Put all ingredients in the goblet and blend until smooth.

MILKY ORANGE DRINK

QUANTITIES for 1 large glass

6 oz orange juice (180 ml): 1 oz dried skimmed milk (25 g): 1 tsp honey

Blend thoroughly and serve at once.

CREAMED TOMATO

QUANTITIES for 1 glass

6 oz chilled tomato juice (180 ml): 1 heaped Tbs dried skimmed milk powder: ¼ – ½ tsp celery salt or paprika pepper to taste: 1 Tbs cream

Blend thoroughly and serve at once.

BANANA MILK SHAKE

QUANTITIES for 1 large or 2 small glasses

8 oz cold milk (200 ml): 1 small ripe banana

Peel the banana and cut it in pieces. Blend all together until smooth.

BANANA AND CHOCOLATE MILK SHAKE

QUANTITIES for 1 large or 2 small glasses

¼ pt milk (150 ml): ½ Tbs cocoa powder: ½ Tbs caster sugar: 1 Tbs desiccated coco-nut: 1 small ripe banana

Peel the banana and cut it in pieces. Put all ingredients in the blender and mix smooth. Serve hot or cold.

LEMON AND HONEY MILK SHAKE

QUANTITIES for 1 large tumbler

1 Tbs lemon juice: ¼ pt chilled milk (150 ml): 1 tsp honey or to taste: 1 Tbs crushed ice

Blend until smooth and frothy. Serve at once.

PRUNE MILK SHAKE

QUANTITIES for 1 large or 2 small glasses

¼ pt cold water (150 ml): 1 heaped Tbs dried skimmed milk powder: 1 tsp honey: 4 – 6 stoned cooked or canned prunes: Strip of yellow lemon rind: 1 tsp cream

Put in the goblet and blend until smooth. Serve at once.

STRAWBERRY MILK SHAKE

QUANTITIES for 1 large glass

6 oz chilled milk (180 ml): Sugar to taste: 2 oz fresh or frozen strawberries (50 g): 1 Tbs cream

If frozen berries are used allow them to thaw slightly and then blend all the ingredients together. Serve at once or keep chilled.

Alternative. Use raspberries, or other berries in place of strawberries.

ORANGE AND COTTAGE CHEESE

QUANTITIES for 1 large or 2 small glasses

6 oz chilled orange juice (180 ml): 1 Tbs cottage cheese

Blend together and serve at once.

BANANA AND COTTAGE CHEESE

QUANTITIES for 2 glasses

¼ pt milk (150 ml): 2 oz cottage cheese (50 g): 1 medium-sized ripe banana: ½ Tbs brown sugar

Peel the banana and cut it in pieces. Put all in the blender and mix until smooth.

TOMATO AND COTTAGE CHEESE

QUANTITIES for 1 glass

¼ pt chilled tomato juice (150 ml): 2 oz cottage cheese (50 g): Pinch of celery salt and additional salt to taste: Paprika pepper or other pepper to taste

Blend until smooth and serve at once.

YOGURT DRINK

This makes ordinary yogurt into a drink like the filmjölk or surmelk of Sweden and Norway.

QUANTITIES for 2 good-sized glasses

½ pt plain yogurt (250 ml): ¼ pt cold milk (150 ml)

Remove both these from the refrigerator just before mixing. Put in the goblet and blend until smooth and frothy. If liked still thinner, add more cold milk.

YOGURT AND FRUIT JUICE

QUANTITIES for 2 small glasses

¼ pt yogurt (150 ml): ¼ pt fruit juice (150 ml): Sugar to taste

Chill yogurt and juice thoroughly before mixing smooth.

YOGURT AND HONEY

QUANTITIES for 2 glasses

½ pt plain yogurt (250 ml): Pinch salt: 1 Tbs lemon juice: 2 tsp honey

Blend together to make smooth and frothy.

TOMATO AND YOGURT

QUANTITIES for 2 small glasses

¼ pt chilled canned tomato juice (150 ml): ¼ pt chilled plain yogurt (150 ml): Salt and pepper: Worcester sauce to taste: Onion, celery or garlic salt

Put in the goblet and blend for a few seconds.

EGG NOGS OR FLIPS

BANANA EGG NOG

QUANTITIES for 1 large or 2 small glasses

1 egg: 1 small ripe banana: ¼ pt single cream (150 ml): 2 Tbs milk: 1 Tbs caster sugar: Vanilla essence

Peel and cut up the banana. Put all ingredients in the goblet and blend thoroughly.

ORANGE EGG NOG

QUANTITIES for 1 large or 2 small glasses

1 egg: 1 Tbs sugar: 6 oz chilled orange juice (180 ml)

Blend until frothy and serve at once.

SHERRY EGG NOG

QUANTITIES for 1 large or 2 small glasses

1 egg: 1 – 2 tsp sugar: 8 oz milk (200 ml): Pinch salt: 1 tsp sherry: Grated nutmeg

The milk may be hot or chilled. Blend all except the nutmeg which is sprinkled on top just before serving.

ICED COFFEE

QUANTITIES for 2 large glasses

1 Tbs soluble coffee: 4 ice cubes, crushed: ½ pt cold water (250 ml): ¼ pt single cream (150 ml): 2 tsp sugar or to taste: 1 tsp brandy, rum, or whisky or ½ tsp vanilla essence

Blend all together until light and frothy and serve at once.

SPICED MOCHA DRINK
(hot or cold)

QUANTITIES for 4 – 6

4 Tbs drinking chocolate: 1 Tbs instant coffee: ½ tsp vanilla or 1 tsp rum: ¼ tsp ground cinnamon: Pinch nutmeg: ¼ pt hot water (150 ml)

Put in the goblet and blend for 30 seconds. Tip into a pan.

¾ *pt milk (375 ml): Whipped cream*

Add the milk and bring to the boil. Serve with a spoonful of cream on top.

To serve cold, process as before in the goblet and then add ice-cold milk or some ice and cold milk. Serve with cream as before.

Chapter Twenty-three

INFANTS AND TODDLERS

A very large number of the small blenders in use were probably purchased initially for making baby foods. There are certain advantages in doing this at home rather than relying entirely upon canned baby and junior foods. The old way of preparing these foods in the home was to sieve the cooked food, a time-consuming job compared with blending. Blended baby foods are usually cheaper, and certainly fresher tasting than the canned variety, an important point in getting a child used to the taste of fresh cooked foods as served in family meals.

There is no need to do special cooking for this. Meat, with gravy or milk, vegetables, and pudding from the family dinner are usually suitable for the child, provided they are blended to a soft consistency.

A warning about food for the toddler; while it saves mother's time if the food is blended rather than cut up by hand, it is not a good plan always to give soft food, otherwise the child becomes lazy about chewing. Give some meals with blended foods and others where chewing is required.

The degree of blending used will depend on the age of the child: thorough blending of meat and vegetables with gravy or milk to make a smooth paste is ideal for the small baby, but shorter blends, just to mince or shred, are more suitable for the toddler. Naturally, what you give the baby will depend on the advice you are given by your family doctor, health visitor or clinic.

Clean equipment is essential in preparing infant foods so wash, rinse, and scald the blender goblet before and after use. This is vital if you are going to use the blender for mixing dried milk and other milky drinks.

When blending meat, vegetables and puddings it is better to do a little each day, as required, so that it is always fresh; although if you are very strict about hygiene in handling the food, it is safe to store some for a day in the refrigerator, longer in the freezer, but green vegetables should be freshly cooked each day for maximum vitamin content.

Useful Foods to Blend for Infants and Toddlers are:

Savoury

Meat from the family dinner, with gravy to moisten. Include some vegetable for the infant but the toddler can chew ordinary ones.

If the meat is not suitable for a young child, blend the vegetables with a meat substitute such as an egg or some pieces of cheese, reheating before serving if necessary. If the vegetables are hot when they go in the blender, this will cook the egg and melt the cheese without re-heating.

For the toddler, use the blender to make meat, fish and cheese fillings for sandwiches for the tea meal. Blend with a little milk and some raw vegetables, just to chop them.

From 18 months onwards raw vegetable salads are suitable if they are chopped small in the blender.

Sweet

Purée canned, stewed or raw fruit and then add rice pudding or custard to make a quick sweet.

Fruit pulp can be set in jelly or used as a sauce for milk puddings, for example, blancmange.

Half a banana blended with a little sugar and a couple of tablespoons of milk makes another quick sweet to use when the family pudding is not suitable. Likewise raw, blended apple with a little sugar and water can be cooked in 10 minutes.

Chapter Twenty-four

SPECIAL DIETS

For many years a blender has been a standard piece of equipment in hospital kitchens to help in the preparation of diets such as the fluid or liquid, semi-solid or soft, and the low-fibre diet, (also known as low-roughage or bland diet).

In addition, the blender helps to introduce variety into other diets such as the low-carbohydrate and diabetic, the low-calorie or reducing diet, the gluten-free diet, and many others.

FLUID OR LIQUID DIETS

Use the blender for mixing all drinks required, which it does in seconds, making them smooth and free from lumps. Blend canned and packet soups to make smooth liquids and blend some with small pieces of cheese or meat to add protein and flavour.

HIGH-PROTEIN MILK

QUANTITIES for 1 large tumbler

8 oz fresh milk (200 ml): 1 oz dried milk powder (low-fat or full-cream) (25 g): Flavouring and sweetening to taste

Put all in the blender goblet and mix for a few seconds. Hot or cold milk can be used according to the type of drink. For really cold drinks to soothe a sore throat, blend a crushed ice cube or some ice cream with the other ingredients.

Flavouring: cocoa, chocolate, soluble coffee, fruit syrups and fruit purées, Ovaltine, Horlick's and other proprietary drinks, Marmite or Bovril, malt extract, and any other flavouring liked by the patient.

BREAKFAST GRUEL
(using a portion from the family porridge made with oats)

1 small portion of hot, cooked porridge: Twice the volume of hot milk: ½ oz low-fat dried milk powder (2 heaped Tbs): Sugar to taste: Cream to taste, if allowed

Put all in the warmed goblet and blend for a few seconds, re-heating before serving if necessary.

QUICK MILK SOUP
(using some fresh-cooked vegetables from the family dinner or use canned or left-overs)

1 small portion of cooked vegetables: ¼ pt hot milk (150 ml), or more as needed to thin the vegetables: Salt and pepper to taste

Put all in the warmed goblet and blend until smooth. Re-heat if necessary.

MEAT AND FISH SOUPS

Lightly cooked and tender meats and cooked fish can be made into soups by blending with hot milk and stock, seasoning to taste and heating. Some vegetables may be included, too, if liked.

EGG BROTH

QUANTITIES for 2 small portions

½ pt meat stock or canned consommé (250 ml): 1 egg: Salt and pepper

Heat the stock or consommé to boiling and put it in the warmed goblet with the egg and seasoning. Blend for a few seconds and serve in a hot cup or soup bowl.

CANNED STRAINED FOODS
(infant or junior)

These are useful emergency stocks for fluids. Simply empty the contents of the can into the blender goblet, add milk or stock and blend to make smooth. Adjust the seasoning and serve hot or cold according to the variety.

FRUIT MOUSSE

Provided they don't contain whole fruit, gelatine sweets can count as fluids because they soften in the mouth and slide down easily.

QUANTITIES for 4

¼ oz gelatine (½ Tbs): 2 Tbs hot water

Dissolve the gelatine in the water

1 lb cold, drained stewed or canned fruit (500 g): Sugar to taste: ¼ pt evaporated milk (150 ml)

Put in the blender goblet with the dissolved gelatine and blend until smooth and light. Tip into a bowl and leave until it just begins to set

1 egg white: 1 Tbs sugar

Beat the egg white until stiff and beat in the sugar. Fold it into the fruit mixture and turn into a serving dish or individual dishes. Chill in the refrigerator before serving.

For Other Recipes Suitable for this Diet, see
Asparagus Soup, Chicken Soup, Carrot Soup, Cold Green Pea
Soup, Cauliflower Soup, Vichyssoise, Celery Soup. Fruit Ice
Cream. Milk, Yogurt and Cottage Cheese Drinks. Mocha Ice
Cream, Egg Nogs and Flips, Yogurt Jelly Whip, Iced Coffee,
Fruit Drinks.

SEMI-SOLID OR SOFT DIETS

All the suggestions for the fluid diet are suitable for this one too.
In addition, some more solid foods may be added. Blender-
grated cheese is useful for sprinkling on soups and savoury
dishes and pieces of cheese can be blended in sauces to serve with
fish and vegetables. All meats, except very tender ones, usually
need to be in the form of a purée or mince. Some from the family
meal can be blended with sauce or gravy to make a suitable
consistency. Most vegetables can be served in this diet and most
need to be pulped. Use some of the freshly cooked family
vegetables and blend them smooth without any added liquid.
Re-heat if necessary.

SWEETENED COTTAGE CHEESE

Blend the cottage cheese to make it smooth, adding a little cream
or evaporated milk, sugar and vanilla to taste. Place a mound of
the cheese in individual dishes and surround with a fresh or
canned fruit purée. Alternatively, put a layer of fruit purée in the
bottom of the dishes and the cheese on top. Garnish with a little
ground cinnamon or grated chocolate.

BAKED CHEESE CUSTARD

COOKING TIME: $\frac{1}{2} - \frac{3}{4}$ hr. TEMPERATURE: E.350°F (180°C) G.4.
or 3 mins. in the pressure cooker.

QUANTITIES for 4

*$\frac{1}{2}$ pt hot milk (250 ml): 4 eggs: $\frac{1}{2}$ oz butter (1 Tbs): Pinch salt,
cayenne and paprika: 3 oz well-flavoured cheese (75 g): 1 tsp pre-
pared mustard*

Grease four individual moulds or cups. Put all the ingredients in
the goblet and mix until smooth. Pour into the moulds and stand

them in a shallow pan of hot water. Bake until set. If the pressure cooker is used, allow the pressure to drop slowly.

Unmould and serve with fingers of toast (bread for the patient), or serve cold with salad for the family or with tomato purée for the patient.

FRUIT FOOL

QUANTITIES for 4

1 lb drained canned or cooked fruit (500 g): Sugar to taste: ¼ pt thick cold custard (150 ml) :¼ pt whipping cream or evaporated milk (150 ml)

Blend the fruit and sugar to a pulp. Add the custard and blend smooth. Add cream or milk and blend again until thick and light. Pour into individual dishes and chill in the refrigerator.

FRUIT MERINGUE

COOKING TIME: 20 mins. TEMPERATURE: E.350°F (180°C) G.4. QUANTITIES for 4

1 lb drained cooked or canned fruit (500 g): Sugar to taste

Blend until a smooth pulp and tip into a bowl.

2 egg whites: 1 oz sugar (25 g)

Beat the egg whites stiff and fold half of them into the fruit. Put in a baking dish. Fold the sugar into the rest of the egg white and pile it on top of the fruit. Bake in a low oven until the meringue is set. Serve cold with cream or a custard sauce made with the egg yolk.

Other Suitable Recipes are:

Savoury
Asparagus Soup, Carrot Soup, Cauliflower Soup, Chicken Soup, Cold Cream of Pea Soup. Scrambled Egg. Chicken Mousse, Ham Mousse. Cold Asparagus Mould. Broad Bean Purée, Carrot Purée, Spinach au Beurre.

Sweet
Apricot Mould, Apricot Fool. Banana Fool, Banana Mousse, Banana Whip. Chocolate and Orange Mould. Fruit Ice Cream. Pain de Fruit. Prune and Pineapple Fool. Yogurt Jelly Whip.

LOW-FIBRE DIET
(low roughage or bland)

The important thing with this diet is to avoid all coarse fibres in food which could act as an irritant to the inflamed intestine. The blender, by breaking up the fibre in food, dividing it into very fine particles, makes blended food very suitable for these diets.

Use the blender for mixing nourishing milk drinks and soups as with the fluid diet; for grating cheese finely to make it easier to digest; to purée fruit, vegetables, jams and marmalades; and for making soft and light puddings.

Suitable Recipes are:

Savoury

Carrot Soup	Fish Mousse
Cauliflower Soup	Fish Mousseline
Chicken Soup	Norwegian Fish Mould
Cold Cream of Pea Soup	Quennelles
Cottage Cheese Omelet	Chicken or Rabbit Timbales
Eggs Crécy	Carrot Purée
Omelet	Spinach au Beurre
Scrambled Egg	Quick Milk Soup
Chicken Mousse	Baked Cheese Custard

Sweet

Apricot Mould	Yogurt Jelly Whip
Chocolate and Orange Mould	Lemon Delicious Pudding
Banana Mould	Queen of Puddings
Banana Mousse	Fruit Mousse
Prune and Pineapple Fool	Sweetened Cottage Cheese
	Fruit Meringue

LOW-CARBOHYDRATE AND
DIABETIC DIETS

A number of the recipes in this book are low-carbohydrate and I give below a list of them, with their carbohydrate content per portion.

The blender is very useful for making good sauces and soups without starchy thickenings and I have included some of these.

Because the general run of puddings are not low-carbohydrate, I include here a few suitable blender recipes for these. The quantities are for four portions because they are palatable enough for all the family. I have not suggested adding sugar substitutes for sweetening because I prefer them without; they can be added if desired, but I think for family use it is better to make them without and then those who must have sweet things (and who are not on the diet), can sprinkle sugar on at table.

Other Suitable Recipes are:

	Per Portion	
	Carbohydrate g.	Calories
Cucumber Soup	negligible	59
Iced Cucumber Soup	negligible	16
Cheese Sauce without Flour	5	180
Whole Egg Hollandaise	negligible	128
Breton Sauce	negligible	130
Viennese Egg Sauce	negligible	136
Cottage Cheese Omelet	negligible	132
Omelet	negligible	122–198
Swiss Eggs	negligible	230
Blue Cheese Mousse	4	227
Emmenthal Mousse	negligible	305
Cheese Soufflé	5	224
Fish and Cheese Soufflé	negligible	176
Fish Shape (without sauce)	8	220
Norwegian Fish Mould	8	304
Chicken and Ham Mould	negligible	146
Chicken or Rabbit Timbales	5	270
Beef and Mushroom Casserole	3	365
Chicken Casserole	3	262

APRICOT DESSERT

COOKING TIME: a few minutes. QUANTITIES for 4: 15 g carbohydrate per portion; 114 Calories.

6 oz cooked dried apricots (170 g): ½ oz cornflour (14 g): 16 oz milk (450 ml)

Blend the ingredients together until smooth. Pour into a pan, stir until boiling and simmer for 2 – 3 minutes.

Almond or lemon essence

Flavour to taste and pour into individual serving dishes. Serve warm or cold.

CINNAMON APPLES

QUANTITIES for 4; 10 g carbohydrate per portion; 40 Calories.

1 lb dessert apples (500 g)

Peel, core and stew the apples until tender, adding only enough water to prevent burning. Put in the goblet.

½ tsp ground cinnamon or to taste

Add to the apples and blend them to a smooth purée. Serve cold in individual glasses.

PRUNE AND ORANGE MOULD

QUANTITIES for 2; 10 g carbohydrate per portion; 97 Calories.

6 oz hot water (180 ml): ¼ oz gelatine (¾ Tbs)

Put the water in the goblet and sprinkle in the gelatine. Blend for a few seconds.

2 eggs

Add to the goblet and blend for 30 seconds.

4 oz cooked prunes, without sugar (125 g), stones removed: 2 Tbs prune juice: 1 tsp lemon juice: 2 strips orange rind

Add to the goblet and blend until smooth and light. Pour into a mould and leave to set.

THE GLUTEN-FREE DIET

The following recipes are gluten-free provided any manufactured foods used in them are also gluten-free. Lists of packet, canned and bottled foods which are gluten-free can be purchased from the Coeliac Society, 116 Loudoun Road, London N.W.8.

Suitable Recipes are:

Patés and Spreads
Cheese and Walnut Spread, Chicken Liver Pâté, Chicken Liver Spread, Egg and Onion Spread, Fish Pâté or Spread, Kipper Pâté or Spread, Mixed Liver Terrine, Potted Duck, Potted Tongue, Salmon and Egg Spread, Sardine and Cheese Spread, Smoked Cod's Roe Spread.

Soups
Asparagus, Carrot, Celery, Cheese and Watercress, Corn, Cucumber, Soupe Flamande, Potato and Onion, Bortsch, Iced Cucumber, Gaspacho, Cold Cream of Pea, Vichyssoise.

Sauces
Celery, Cheese (without flour), Fish Roe, Hollandaise, Breton, Creamed Cheese Dressing, English Salad Dressing, Mayonnaise, Rich Mustard Sauce, Viennese Egg Sauce, Banana Sauce, Cherry, Chocolate, Quick Chocolate, Custard, Raw Fruit Sauce, Cooked Fruit Sauce, Jam Sauce, Marmalade Sauce, Jelly Sauce, Lemon or Orange Sauce, Melba Sauce.

Eggs Meat and Fish
Cottage Cheese Omelet, Swiss Eggs, Chicken Mousse, Fish Mousse, Ham Mousse, Fish Mousseline, Norwegian Fish Mould, Quenelles, Fish Créole, Chicken and Ham Mould, Braised Beef, Chicken in Green Tarragon Sauce, Lamb Cutlets with Yogurt Sauce, Pork in Sour Sweet Sauce, Veal and Ham Blanquette.

Vegetables
Cold Asparagus Mould, Dolmas, Carrot Mould with Green Peas, Green Pea Purée with Eggs and Bacon.

Sweets, Puddings and Cakes
Apple Fool, Apricot Mould, Apricot Purée with Almonds, Apricot Fool, Banana Mould with Strawberry Sauce, Banana Mousse, Banana Whip, Coffee Bavarois, Coffee Cheese Cream, Fruit Ice Cream, Hazel Nut Ice Cream, Marmalade de Pruneaux, Baked Banana Mousse, Baked Soufflé Omelet, Almond Macaroons, Austrian Hazel Nut Gâteau, Hazel Nut Cookies.

RECIPE INDEX

171